TOP DOLLAR PAID!
The Complete Guide to Selling Your Stamps

STEPHEN R. DATZ

GENERAL PHILATELIC CORPORATION
LOVELAND, COLORADO

PRINTING HISTORY
First Edition
First printing: August 1989
Second printing: March 1990
Third printing: January 1992

Second Edition
First printing: December 1996
Second printing: September 1997
Third printing: August 2003

ISBN: 0-88219-022-9

Cover design: Mike Jenson
Manufactured in the United States of America.

Published by General Philatelic Corporation
Division of General Trade Corporation
Post Office Box 402
Loveland, CO 80539
(970) 667-1133

Philatelic Books by Stephen R. Datz

THE BUYER'S GUIDE

THE DATZ PHILATELIC INDEX

ERRORS ON U.S. STAMPS

ON THE ROAD

STAMP COLLECTING

THE STAMP COLLECTOR'S BIBLE

STAMP INVESTING

TOP DOLLAR PAID

THE WILD SIDE

CONTENTS

ACKNOWLEDGMENTS

The anecdotal episodes portrayed in this book are based on actual incidents. In most cases, names and details have been changed to protect individual privacy. Thanks are due John Hotchner for generously taking the time to work with the manuscript and offer suggestions and criticisms, which were immensely helpful. Thanks are also due Bob Dumaine and Jacques Schiff Jr. for sharing their insights into the fascinating world of error stamps. I am very grateful to Jim Magruder for his expertise, assistance, and encouragement. Thanks to Keith Harmer for kind permission to reproduce the illustration of gum and hinging. Thanks to Robin Quinn for copy editing and proofreading. Thanks to my wife, Susan, for proofreading and suggestions, but most of all for her patience during preparation of this book and during all our years in business. And thanks are due all the sellers of stamps who, over the years, provided me with the experiences that are the basis for this book.

FOREWORD

The title of this book, *Top Dollar Paid!*, was not chosen by accident. It is, without doubt, the most overworked cliché in the stamp trade. Top dollar offers scream from headlines atop buying ads which, if neon, would flash: *Top Cash Prices Paid!, Top $$$$, Best Prices Paid!, The Higher Buyer!, We Will Not Be Outbid!, All Offers Topped!, We Buy It All!, Immediate Cash!, One of America's Largest Buyers!, One of the World's Largest Buyers!, Why Take Less?* There seems to be no limit to the creative headlines. But regardless of the phrasing, the message is the same: *"We want your stamps!"*

Trite as they may sound, the insistent entreaties point out an important element of the stamp industry: dealers must buy stamp collections in order to maintain their stocks. Unlike other retailers, stamp dealers cannot pick up the telephone and order more from the factory when they run low on inventory. That fact of economic life creates a highly competitive market and assures sellers that they *will* get top dollar if they approach the business of selling knowledgeably. And that's what this book is all about!

Stamp collections are formed over a period of years, the result of numerous transactions. But the sale of a collection typically occurs only once and is the single most important stamp transaction in a collector's life. It's a task for which few sellers are prepared, one usually approached with trepidation rather than anticipation. Yet it need not be that way. What follows is a journey through the process of selling as seen from the stamp dealer's perspective. The idea is to remove some of the mystery surrounding selling and give you a better idea of how to approach the task.

At first glance, it would appear that the stamp dealer has all the advantages: knowledge, experience, and skill. He buys and sells stamps every day and knows the market intimately. The seller would seem to be at a tremendous disadvantage. He enters the arena with trepidation, sure that the wily dealer will get the best of the deal. In reality, the seller too has as much going for him; he just isn't aware of it. The seller's edge is that he calls the shots. He decides when and if he will sell, and to whom he will sell. He can shop for as many offers as he wants. He can walk away from a potential deal at any time and start over somewhere else. Or he can choose not to sell and sit tight. The seller controls the situation; that is his big edge.

The purpose of this book is twofold: to inform the seller how to go about his task, and to entertain. This approach is intended to make the selling experience less intimidating and more profitable. The idea came to me one day after having spent an inordinately long time trying to explain to a seller how stamp values are determined, how the stamp market works, and how stamp dealers arrive at offers. When I had finished, I thought, *I could have written a book on the subject.* And the more I thought about it, the more it made sense to do just that.

There's no reason why the seller shouldn't come to the bargaining table informed. After all, any dealer will tell you that it's easier to do business with someone who knows what he's got and understands the market than with someone who has no idea of what he has. The informed seller is able to recognize a fair offer and act on it. The uninformed seller thrashes around in the dark closet of doubt and indecision, never quite sure if he should accept an offer or not.

At first I thought about just giving the essentials in guide form, but my own experience with how-to books is that no matter how clearly the facts have been recited, it takes experience to gain proficiency. Selling a stamp collection is usually a once in a lifetime event, so there is little opportunity to gain experience. I felt that it would be helpful to put you—the potential seller—behind the counter with me. By sharing my experiences, you will gain a better understanding of what is involved in the selling transaction. And if you still actively collect, you may even learn something about the financial consequences of your particular collecting habits.

I have traveled countless thousands of miles, looked at thousands of collections, and listened to thousands of stories from collectors. I have found the people to be just as interesting as the stamps, and often, more so. When you mix stamps and people together, and spice liberally with money, the result is a stew as rich in drama as any conceived by a novelist or screenwriter. The personalities in this book, their dreams of treasure, their joys and disappointments, their greed, suspicion and mistrust, their generosity and kindness, and their occasional poverty and tragedy are not the stuff of fiction; they are real.

So come along, watch over my shoulder, and see what it's all about. You'll meet some characters. You'll learn how a dealer values a collection, what appeals to him and what doesn't, and hopefully you'll come away with knowledge that you can utilize in your quest to get top dollar for your stamps. And I hope that you'll have a good time doing it!

THE STAMP DEALER'S ROLE

The stamp dealer's role is central to the stamp market: he provides liquidity, makes it possible to convert your stamp collection into cash. Without the stamp dealer acting as go-between, the market would be terribly disorganized and stamp prices would suffer accordingly. Think of the poor matchbook cover collector. His collection is both highly illiquid and of questionable value because there are few, if any, dealers and no organized market.

The stamp dealer acts as a bridge between buyer and seller. He buys entire collections for cash on the spot, then assumes the task of finding homes for all the stamps. He accomplishes this service by setting up shop, by advertising, by establishing a clientele for a wide variety of material, and by being willing to bear the cost of inventorying stamps for which he has no immediate sale. For performing this service he expects to be paid, and that payment comes in the form of profit.

The stamp dealer buys at one price and sells at another. The difference is known as a markup. Unfortunately, he does not get to keep the entire markup; markup is not the same as profit. There are expenses to be paid: rent, advertising, utilities, telephone, insurance, operating supplies, employee costs, taxes, and so on. The remainder after expenses is net profit. That net profit represents the fee paid to the dealer by the market for his services, for taking his time and trouble, and for risking his capital to facilitate the transfer of stamps from those who no longer want them to those who do. Fundamental as it may seem, many people don't understand the role the dealer plays or the degree of profit he must build into his transactions in order to continue in that role.

All too often dealers take abuse from sellers who can't seem to understand that the markup between a $600 offer and a $1,000 retail price is not pure profit. Of the markup, as much as $300 will go toward expenses—the direct costs of maintaining the business that permits a seller to walk in at any given time with stamps and walk out with cash in hand. The remaining $100 profit is the actual net fee the dealer retains for his trouble.

Before we go any further, you must understand this fundamental fact of economic life: *there must be a sizable difference between what dealers pay for stamps and what they charge for stamps.*

SELECTING A DEALER

Selecting the right dealer is vital to getting the best price. Locate dealers through the following sources: the Yellow Pages, stamp newspapers and magazines, philatelic society journals, advertisements in stamp catalogues, a stamp collector acquaintance, or an organization such as the American Stamp Dealers Association (ASDA). Philatelic periodicals and stamp society journals—such as the *American Philatelist* (the journal of the American Philatelic Society)—are especially useful in locating dealers who specialize in specific countries or areas. Examples of specialties include things such as error stamps; German, French or Brazilian stamps; civil war stamps and covers; etc. A list of periodicals appears in the Appendix.

Reliability is the most important quality to look for in a dealer. Don't hesitate to ask for references: bank references, business references, collector references, and professional credentials. In my opinion, the most important indicators of reliability are length of time in business, size and general reputation of the dealer, and professional associations such as membership in the ASDA.

The ASDA is the oldest and the most respected professional organization of stamp dealers. Membership is restricted exclusively to stamp dealers. Applicants are carefully scrutinized before being admitted. In addition to providing general and financial references, applicants must have been in the stamp business for a minimum number of years and must agree to conduct themselves according to a strict code of ethics.

Of real benefit to the seller is that all ASDA members must answer complaints made against them or face expulsion. Recourse through ASDA is an important safeguard to the uninformed seller. The ASDA can be a powerful ally in the event of a dispute. However, the power of the ASDA to enforce its standards applies only to those dealers who are members. It cannot take action against dealers who are not members.

The ASDA will provide upon request a list of stamp dealer members in your area. The ASDA also maintains a list of dealers who have been expelled for unethical business practices. The address of the ASDA is listed in the Appendix.

The other important quality you should look for in a dealer is familiarity with the type of stamps you have for sale. Almost any dealer will be able to help you with a general collection—either U.S. or worldwide. However, if your collection consists of specialized material, contact a dealer who specializes in that type of material. A specialist is the best market for stamps in his field.

Be aware that all stamp dealers are not alike. Each buys according to his own needs and circumstances. The small, local dealer may not be the best market for great rarities. By the same token, the dealer who caters to a selective, high-ticket clientele may not be the best market for a typical, modest collection. A specialist in stamps of the Far East is not likely to be the best market for stamps of Peru.

Many circumstances influence a dealer's buying habits: his size, location, market, capital, clientele, and specialty. More about this topic in the chapter "Appraisals and Offers." If you are unfamiliar with stamps, look for a dealer who is friendly and willing to share information. Don't be afraid to ask questions.

In summary, select a reliable dealer. Don't hesitate to check references. And remember, a specialist is the best market for stamps in his field.

METHODS OF SALE

Methods of selling your stamps include: outright sale, auction, consignment, private treaty arrangement, and so forth. Each has advantages and disadvantages.

Outright sale. Outright sale is the most direct and simple way to dispose of stamps. Once a price is agreed upon, settlement is immediate; you walk away with cash in hand.

Auction. Sale by auction is popular. The auction commission is usually ten percent of the hammer price (i.e. the highest bid) but can vary up or down depending on the size of the consignment. Each auction house has its own fee schedule. Major auction houses require minimum consignments of at least $1,000 net value (the amount they expect the stamps to yield when auctioned). Low profit margins make it uneconomical for them to handle smaller consignments. Many auctions offer advances. More detailed information appears in the following chapter.

Private treaty. In a private treaty arrangement the stamp dealer acts in the capacity of agent or broker. Collections offered by private treaty are typically sold intact and privately, often by the dealer by special mailings or telephone calls to select clients. Commissions are negotiable and vary depending upon the size and type of collection.

Consignment for retail. In some cases, a dealer will take stamps on consignment. Typically, he pays as the stamps sell.

You should agree in advance on the minimum price for each item, rate of commission, and terms for payout. Make sure you get an agreement in writing, and make a photocopies of your stamps or album pages to avoid the possibility of confusion or disagreement later on. Make sure the dealer has insurance and that it will cover your stamps. Your written agreement should state the insurance value covered in case of loss.

Listen to the dealer's advice about pricing. Stamps priced unrealistically high only sit around. You're wasting your time if you expect retail buyers to pay more for your material than it's worth. That's not the way the competitive market works.

Before entering into any consignment agreement, make sure that the dealer is reliable and has been established for a number of years. Be suspicious of any dealer who tries to persuade you to leave your stamps on consignment *rather* than take cash, *while at the same time* promising to get you unrealistically high prices. This approach is often the sign of an undercapitalized operation. You don't want to be left holding the bag the shoe-string operation goes out of business.

The advantages to consignment are that the seller has a voice in setting prices and the potential for higher yields exists.

The disadvantages are that money comes in slowly over a period of time and only the better items tend to sell. Consignment is not advised for the novice.

Stamp shows. Stamp shows range in size from small local events with 20 or so booths to international extravaganzas featuring several hundred booths. The concentration of dealers in one place offers an excellent opportunity to get a variety of opinions, which is especially useful for those new to stamps. You can chat with dealers, ask questions, and get as many offers as you want. You'll quickly learn the real cash value of your stamps.

You can meet both local dealers and those from out of town. Rosters of dealers are usually available from show sponsors weeks before the show. Don't expect dealers to give you their full attention during prime time (late Friday afternoon and all day Saturday). They're usually swamped with retail customers at those times and do not like to be distracted. The best times to meet with dealers are early Friday and Sunday mornings.

If your collection is too large to haul to the show, contact a dealer about coming to your home to view it. But don't wait until the weekend of the show to make an appointment; dealers tend to get booked up. Call well in advance. Information on upcoming stamp shows in your area is available in the stamp weeklies and the *American Philatelist.* Or check with a local dealer about scheduled shows.

Retailing your stamps. In order to sell stamps directly to the public, you must advertise, visit stamp clubs, take booths at stamp shows, or adopt some other retail strategy. It must be said at the outset: retailing is a thankless task. If your motive is to convert your stamps into cash and be done with it, assuming the role of stamp dealer is not the way to go about it.

The advantages of retail sale are that you set the asking prices and you retain all profits. The drawbacks are numerous.

Retailing takes a lot of time. You must identify the stamps, prepare them for sale, price them, and then make the sales. Liquidating an entire collection often takes months or longer. Retail buyers tend to be picky. They buy only what they actually need for their collections. Advertising is costly. You'll waste money learning that the local newspaper doesn't pull the kind of clientele you had in mind. Instead, you'll meet lots of lookers and bargain hunters, perhaps even an unsavory character casing your operation—but few buyers.

Mail-order selling is not as easy as it looks either. You'll learn that philatelic publications generate multiple orders for the choicest items while the majority remain unsold. You'll be amazed at the number of fussy buyers who disagree with your descriptions or grading and demand refunds. You'll also have to make refunds for items sold out. You'll quickly discover that mail-order stamp dealing involves lots of correspondence.

Advertising contains other pitfalls. You may inadvertently price your material too high and get no response. Nothing is more discouraging. You'll discover that many buyers are reluctant to do business with new and unfamiliar dealers. You'll make all the mistakes newcomers make, the kind that established dealers made early on. You'll discover that undertaking any new business involves a steep learning curve—there are dues to be paid.

In my experience, most individuals who try to retail their own stamps eventually throw up their hands in despair. They discover that the gross margin (markup) is not all theirs to keep, that retailing involves a multitude of costs—not the least of which is time. Selling stamps at retail is neither as simple nor as profitable as it may appear at first glance. It's tough to try to be a part-time pro. In most cases, the do-it-yourselfer would be money ahead to sell outright to a dealer.

Internet Selling. Some collectors try selling stamps online, usually through an auction such as eBay. Amateurs often overgrade listings and sometimes misidentify them. As a result, potential buyers tend not to bid as liberally (and often downright parsimoniously) for stamps offered by vendors who are not recognized professionals. New sellers and those with low feedback ratings tend to receive defensive bids. On the other hand, if you are experienced in online selling, Internet auctions can be rewarding.

Donation. If your collection is of little interest to dealers or you are looking for a tax benefit, consider donating it to Stamps for the Wounded (which serves 11,000 individual patients and 56 organized stamp clubs in Veterans hospitals and convalescent centers nationwide), the Salvation Army, the Boy Scouts or Girl Scouts, or other charitable organization. According to IRS rules at the time of this writing, if the value of a donation is less than $500, you won't have to itemize it separately on your tax return. However, you are required to be able to document its value. Check with your accountant for the latest rules.

Gift. Last but not least is the option of making a gift of your stamps. This is especially appropriate if they have little market value but lots of eye appeal. Most of us know youngsters who would consider an old album or accumulation to be a treasure far out of proportion to its market value.

STAMP AUCTIONS

Selling at auction can be an excellent means of turning stamps into cash. Auction is appealing because offer sellers direct access to that market. It brings stamps directly to interested, qualified buyers who bid competitively for the right to own them. When the hammer falls, the lot goes to the person willing to pay the highest price for it. The real cash value of a stamp is thus established. Stamp auctions take place every week all over America, and the fact that stamps of similar type and quality tend to sell for similar prices reflects a stable and orderly market.

Of all the methods of selling, auction is perhaps the most misunderstood. Often, even experienced collectors do not have a clear understanding the auction process. Logic dictates that the best price is realized by selling directly to the public, bypassing the middleman. Nevertheless, sellers often regard auctions as risky. They fear that their stamps might sell for only cents on the dollar, this despite the fact that auction creates the ideal situation they desire—bringing their stamps directly to the buying public.

It is illogical to believe that your stamps are highly desirable, while at the same time fear that they will bring only low prices at auction. In reality, potential buyers compete fiercely for the right to own desirable stamps—those in good condition, those popular with collectors. Desirable stamps fetch good prices!

Paradoxically, the same individual who fears he will receive too little for his stamps at auction tends to avoid buying at auction because he believes he will pay too much. Sometime back, a long-time customer showed up at one of my auctions.

"I'll sign up for a bidder card, but I doubt that I'll be buying anything," he said. "This is my first auction." He looked somewhat apprehensive and unsure of himself. Once the auction got underway, I was surprised to see his hand go up again and again. He turned out to be one of the more spirited bidders, buying a couple dozen lots during the course of the afternoon. After the sale, as he paid for his lots, he remarked that the auction had been fun, that he had found many stamps he needed, and that he felt he had obtained them at reasonable prices.

Does that mean that the stamps sold too cheaply? Not at all. Later, after all the bids had been totaled, I was surprised to discover that the sale grossed nearly 35 percent more than I had estimated. Those who had consigned stamps were sure to be pleased by settlement checks larger than they expected; buyers too had gone home happy. Everyone was satisfied.

My experience has been that auctions serve both buyer and seller well. Only those with unrealistic expectations about the value of their stamps tend to be disappointed.

Auction is not right for every stamp. It will not work magic on common, low-priced stamps—the kind that clutter dealers' back rooms or lie eternally hibernating in collectors' closets. Common stamps will not yield magically high prices by being offered at auction. Medium-to-high grade stamps do the best at auction, as do rarities. Genuinely rare stamps—the kind that come to market only infrequently—often set price records at auction. You can best determine the suitability of your collection for auction by checking with an auction firm.

Most auctions have consignment minimums, typically $1,000 net yield, although it varies from firm to firm. Narrow profit margins make it uneconomical to handle small consignments. If your collection doesn't meet the minimum, chances are that it would not do well at auction anyway.

Those unfamiliar with the stamp trade often assume that stamp auctions are run like local estate or furniture auctions, with lots of bluster and blabber. In fact, stamp auctions are highly sophisticated. First-class auction firms carefully describe and, in many cases, illustrate lots in appealing catalogues, which are mailed to customer lists often containing at least several thousand names. Many of the recipients bid by mail. Floor bidders also compete.

Each auction consignment is lotted (subdivided into individual lots for auction) according to its merits. Stamps of substantial value are described and illustrated separately. The costs of lotting, publishing, mailing, and overhead make it uneconomical to lot individual stamps whose value is less than $50 to $100. Minimums vary from firm to firm. Stamps not meeting the individual lot minimum are grouped into lots commonly referred to as remainders or balances; however, stamps of different consignors are never commingled.

Many auction firms offer cash advances, typically about 50 percent of the expected net yield. Some charge interest on advances; others do not. Some add a percentage point or two to the commission in lieu of interest. An advance enables the seller to have some immediate cash, while at the same time affording the opportunity to realize a yield greater than might otherwise be obtained from outright sale.

Reputable auction firms give realistic estimates of expected yields for collections. A realistic estimate is important; you don't want an unpleasant surprise later on. Be suspicious of any firm that promises an unrealistically high yield to secure your consignment. You will only be disappointed later.

Many consignors, especially inexperienced ones, request reserves (the minimum price below which a lot will not be sold) on lots because they fear that their stamps might sell too cheaply. Some auction firms allow reserves; others do not. The fact is that lots with unrealistic reserves simply fail to attract bids. Overall, reserves simply do not increase yield. As long as you're satisfied with the aggregate net yield quoted in the estimate (which is why it is so important to get a *realistic* estimate), don't waste time worrying about the price realized for each individual lot. In any given auction, some lots sell for less than expected and others for more, but overall they tend to average out. Be concerned only with the estimated aggregate yield for the collection. If you don't like the size of the estimate, don't consign.

Auctions that allow reserves usually charge for them. Others simply advise you to bid on your own lots if you want to protect them. In such cases, you will be charged at least the seller's commission (usually 10 percent) for lots you buy back, and in some instances, the buyer's premium (10 to 15 percent) as well. Charging for reserves is not unreasonable. Auctions do the same amount of work and incur the same expenses whether lots are reserved or unreserved. An auction catalogue containing 1,000 lots can easily cost $10,000 to produce. Simple mathematics shows that each lot costs $10 to offer. Add postage and overhead, and the actual cost is closer to $20 per lot. The combined buyer's and seller's commission on a $100 hammer price is only $20, or break-even. Auctions can't afford to hold sales and not sell lots. Occasionally an auction will agree to no-fee, blanket reserves. Typically, they are new to the auction business or desperate for material. The reserves, an incentive to attract consignors, usually turn out to be an exercise in futility for both seller and auction alike. Their mailing lists are usually not sufficiently developed to generate the kind of high-dollar bids necessary for the strategy to succeed. So the seller gets back most of his material and the auction loses the cost of offering the lots. Established auctions do not encourage reserves because, more often than not, those who insist on them have unrealistically high opinions of their stamps' value.

If you have a specialized collection, seek out an auction firm with an established clientele for that type of material. You won't get the best price for classic U.S. stamps, proofs and essays, or major errors through an auction firm that specializes in foreign stamps. The same applies to foreign stamps offered at auction by a firm that normally handles only U.S. stamps.

When shopping for an auction firm, ask to see catalogues and prices realized for several recent sales in order to get an idea of how your stamps will be presented and how much similar stamps have sold for in previous sales. Ask how your material will be lotted and when it will be offered. Ask to speak to former consignors. Find out if they were satisfied with the results.

If you choose auction, consign your stamps in a timely fashion. Many consignors make the mistake of waiting until the last moment before a deadline. Lot describers are under a lot of pressure at deadline and your stamps may not get the same careful attention they might have received had they been consigned early on. One more tip: experienced consignors often prefer to have their material appear in fall or winter auctions when collector interest is at its highest.

Sale by auction has some drawbacks. The result is not immediate. Typically the time from consignment to settlement is four to six months. Auctions allow at least a month to write up lots. Another two to four weeks are required for catalogue printing and preparation for mailing. Finally, catalogues are mailed three to four weeks in advance of the sale date to allow mail bidders plenty of time to send in bids. After an auction, most firms allow 30 to 45 days to ship lots to successful mail bidders and wait for payments.

Successful bidders are normally permitted to have stamps expertized if they so desire. Payments for lots submitted for expertizing are not disbursed to consignors until those lots have been returned with good expert certificates. Auction firms usually correctly identify stamps when lotting; the risk to the consignor of having a stamp that has been submitted for expert opinion returned is small. Still, the time involved delays payment.

Another drawback to auction is that the consignor assumes the market risk. In the time between consignment and settlement, market prices may rise or fall. Drastic fluctuations rarely occur; still the element of uncertainty exists.

Foreign auctions offer yet another avenue—for the right property. Stamps are usually most in demand in the nation of their origin. German and Swiss auctions advertise heavily in the United States for consignments. They can get tremendous prices for top-quality, specialized material native to their locale. However, foreign auctions tend to be very selective. The key adjectives are *scarce, top-quality,* and *specialized.* Unless you have a specialized, high-dollar property, a foreign auction probably won't be interested.

When consigning abroad, go in with your eyes open; terms and conditions vary from nation to nation. Some foreign auctions charge lotting and illustration fees. You may encounter insurance and special tax fees typically not encountered in U.S. auctions. Also, remember that in case of disagreement, your stamps are outside United States jurisdiction and beyond easy legal recourse. And one more thing, don't consign U.S. stamps to foreign auctions. The best market for U.S. stamps is in the United States.

In summary, auctions offer direct access to the market. Auction is not as simple or as quick as outright sale, but the extra yield tends to offset the extra time involved. For the right stamps and the patient individual, auction is one of the best ways to get top dollar. If you think your collection has auction potential, check with an established stamp auctioneer.

CONDITION, CONDITION, CONDITION

Realtors are fond of saying that the three most important elements of value for a property are "Location, location, location." The question of rarity aside, the three most important elements of value for a given stamp are "Condition, condition, condition." Ninety percent of the price for a superb, mint $5 Columbian priced at $5,000 represents a premium for condition. The exact same stamp might be had for perhaps $500 in seriously faulty condition; $4,500 less than the superb gem. *Condition is the most important attribute of stamp value.*

A word of caution before we go any further. If you are a newcomer to the field of stamp collecting, *don't tamper with your stamps.* Old stamps are fragile. Trying to improve their appearance is very risky. You're likely to damage them, even if you think you're being careful. Don't remove stamps from envelopes or postcards; the intact item may have considerably more value—by virtue of its postmark or other markings—than just the stamps alone. And for the same reason, don't cut the corners off old envelopes. Don't attempt to separate stamps that are stuck together or stuck down to album pages; you'll only cause damage and reduce their value. Don't attempt to clean stamps; you'll do more harm than good. Leave everything intact. Rely on an experienced professional to give you the best advice on how to proceed.

A given stamp is either sound or faulty; that is the first test. A sound stamp is free of faults. Sound stamps are graded according to condition. Grades range from "average" to "superb." Faulty stamps, however, go directly to the lowest price bracket. Grades of condition that might otherwise apply to a sound stamp do not apply to a faulty stamp.

Many kinds of faults exist: tears, thins, pinholes, creases, surface abrasions, stains—anything that might be construed as damage. Thins are usually the result of careless hinge removal (hinges are small bits of paper or glassine used to attach stamps to album pages) and are visible from the back. Creases may be visible to the naked eye, or visible only in watermark fluid (special fluid used for detecting watermarks in paper); either way, they're considered faults. Cellophane tape staining, fading, foxing, or any other discoloration puts a stamp in the faulty category. And stamps that have been repaired are considered faulty nonetheless. Faulty stamps are worth only a small fraction of catalogue value. The precise amount depends on the degree of the fault. Stamps with pieces missing are virtually worthless.

Other elements that are technically not faults, such as straight-edges (collectors prefer stamps with perforations on all four sides, except in the case of coil stamps and imperforates), heavy cancels, and exceedingly poor centering, nevertheless, reduce the value of a stamp to a small fraction of catalogue value.

Stamps that have been regummed, reperforated, or in any other way "restored" are worth considerably less than their "unrestored" counterparts. Regumming is a process intended to improve the appearance of a stamp by applying new gum to simulate original gum. Reperforating is a process of adding perforations to improve the appearance of a straight-edged stamp, or to improve centering by trimming a margin and adding perforations.

Hinging is another factor of value. Contemporary collectors prefer never-hinged (NH) stamps. Until the middle of the twentieth century, stamps were customarily mounted with hinges, which is why so few early stamps survive without hinge marks. Early hinges were often just regular bits of paper attached with whatever glue was handy. They were difficult to remove, often causing thins when pulled off. Later, glassine hinges coated with light adhesives were developed. Glassine hinges are much less likely to cause damage when removed; nevertheless, they still leave hinge marks. The hobby has become increasingly condition conscious, and with the advent of plastic mounts, hinges have fallen into disfavor. Today, collectors want the best, most pristine examples possible, and that means NH stamps. Although a lightly-hinged stamp is not considered faulty, it is less desirable than an NH stamp. As a result, NH stamps command a premium; hinged stamps sell for a discount.

The auction firm Harmers of New York, Inc. uses the illustrations and terminology appearing in Figure 1 to define states of gum on the stamps appearing in its auctions.

GUM

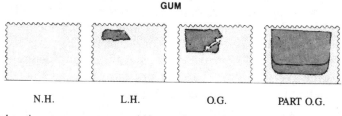

N.H.	L.H.	O.G.	PART O.G.

Shaded portion can represent an actual hinge or the area disturbed by a hinge.

n.h.	=	Never hinged—unused with original gum in Post Office state and unmounted.
l.h.	=	Lightly hinged—unused with full original gum showing some evidence of previous hinge which may be present in part or entirely removed.
o.g.	=	Original gum—unused with original gum somewhat disturbed by previous hinging which may still be present.
o.g. (h.r.)	=	Original gum with hinge remnant
part o.g.	=	Part original gum—unused with original gum, large hinge remnants may or may not be present
disturbed o.g.	=	Disturbed original gum—unused with original gum, affected by sweating, glazing or mount disturbance; may not resemble the original gum.
unused	=	Unused without gum (unless gum is mentioned).
ungummed	=	Unused without gum, as issued.

Figure 1. Gum and hinging. *Courtesy of Harmers of New York, Inc.*

Figure 2. Standard centering grades from left to right include: average; fine; fine to very fine; very fine; and extremely fine.

Grade refers primarily to as stamp's centering and, to a lesser degree, its general appearance. Stamps are priced according to grade. Standard grades include superb (perfect), extremely fine (well centered), very fine (moderately centered), fine (poorly centered), and average (very poorly centered). These grades are illustrated in Figure 2. A variety of split grades, such as F-VF (fine to very fine), describe finer shadings. Catalogues typically list prices for only one or two grades, usually in the middle of the spectrum. Therefore the actual price of a given stamp may be higher or lower, depending on its exact grade.

A philatelic term can have a specific meaning within the hobby while its counterpart in common usage has an altogether different meaning. For example, the term "fine," as applied to stamp centering, has come to mean a poorly centered stamp. To be precise, its perforations need only clear the design; in reality, "fine" stamps are very unattractive. Yet in common usage "fine" refers to something of higher quality than normally encountered. In fact, *Webster's New World Dictionary* defines "fine" as something that is "excellent" or "of superior quality."

Because of the variance in meanings, dealers are used to hearing stamps unintentionally misdescribed. For that reason, telephone estimates are rarely given. The only way a dealer can be sure of condition and grade is to actually see the stamps.

Even when a telephone description sounds explicit, when it sounds as if there is no possible room for misunderstanding, buyer and seller can be worlds apart. I recall an example of just how wide that chasm can be. It began with a telephone call.

"I have a couple of brown stamps with swastikas superimposed on palm trees. Would you be interested in buying them?" the phone caller asked.

"Yes, if they're genuine," I replied. The stamps he described were used by the German Afrika Korps during World War II. They are not listed in the *Scott Catalogue*, however they are listed in the *Michel Catalogue* published in Germany. Numerous forgeries exist.

"Oh, they're genuine all right," he assured me, "My uncle took them off a German soldier in North Africa." *Perhaps,* I thought with a cynicism born of having heard and been taken in by too many stories over the years. Still, I had no concrete reason to disbelieve him. "How much are they worth?" he asked.

"That depends on their condition. I'd need to see them."

"Oh, they're in excellent condition—just like new," the caller replied without hesitation. "Can't you give me a ballpark figure?"

"I don't like to quote over the phone. Too much chance for misunderstanding. I'd really need to see the stamps before I can quote a firm price."

"Hey, I live thirty miles from town. I don't want to make the drive if they're not worth anything. Can't you give me some idea?"

The term "like new" sounded promising, much more so than the term "excellent," which I had heard misapplied to some pretty sorry stamps. So I did something I rarely do; I talked price on the phone. "If they're as nice as you say, perhaps fifty to two hundred dollars, depending on variety and condition. That's not an offer," I emphasized, "just an estimate. I've got to see the stamps before I can quote a firm price."

"Okay," he said. "I'll bring them right over."

"Remember, that price is not an offer. From what you've said, I gather the stamps are like new, fresh as the day they were printed, and completely free of damage. If they're faulty, they won't be worth anywhere near as much as I mentioned."

"Oh, they're nice all right," he insisted. "They've been kept in plastic all these years." The caller's description left me with an image of flawless, top-quality stamps, housed in plastic mounts.

The man arrived in short order. He pulled a bulging, well-worn billfold from his pocket, and from the mass of cards and papers within, extracted two Afrika Korps stamps. They had, indeed, been kept in plastic, a plastic wallet sleeve right next to his driver's license. Over the years they had succumbed to that gentle friction that rubs, scuffs, and tenderizes all wallet papers. They were in terrible condition. One suffered from a bent corner that seemed to hang on by its fingernails, and the other was nearly rubbed through in one spot. I wondered by what reasonably objective standard the seller could possibly have concluded that they were in excellent condition. They were, in fact, critically wounded.

Attempting to explain the concept of "excellent" would have been a waste of time; the man already had his own standard. Instead, I pulled a pristine stamp from a stockbook and placed it beside his stamps.

"This is excellent," I said. "When you told me your stamps were like new, I assumed that they were near perfect: fresh, undamaged, gum intact, no folds, no creases, no bends, no scuffs—as nice as the day they were printed. Unfortunately, your stamps are in very poor condition. I'm sorry, but I can't use them. They're just not of collectible quality."

"I thought you said they were worth fifty to two hundred dollars."

Telephone callers inevitably remember figures but somehow forget condition qualifiers no matter how much they were stressed. "If they were like new. That's what I said—remember? But they're not like new. They're not even salable."

"They look okay to me," he snorted. Then, disappointed, he returned the stamps to his wallet—right back to the very same spot, where they would undoubtedly remain for the next 40 years or until they disintegrated. In the meantime, the story of how they had been liberated from an unfortunate German soldier would take its place in family lore to be retold each time the stamps were shown. And when the time came to pass the stamps to the next generation, the recipient would be told that they would be valuable someday; it was only a matter of time. Thus it would left to the next custodian to discover that age cannot restore what poor condition has taken; time cannot heal some wounds.

In summary, condition is the key factor of value. Sound stamps are priced according to grade. Faulty stamps sell at a substantial discount from catalogue value. Severely impaired stamps are virtually worthless.

HOW STAMPS ARE VALUED

THE FUNDAMENTALS

The purpose of this chapter is to give an overview of stamp pricing, addressing some of the points that those unfamiliar with stamps tend to find confusing. First, let's review the fundamentals: the role of the catalogue and the stamp market on values. Then we'll look at how dealers approach the task of valuing a specific property.

A stamp catalogue is usually the first place a seller turns to get an idea of value. It is the single, most-useful basic reference. Scott Publishing Company publishes a multi-volume set of catalogues that lists, illustrates, and prices virtually every recognized postage stamp in the world. Scott also publishes a specialized catalogue for United States stamps that includes not only postage stamps but a wide range of other items such as Christmas seals, duck-hunting stamps, revenue stamps, locals, and many others. In addition to the Scott catalogues, a variety of foreign catalogues published abroad exists. They are excellent references for stamps of their native lands. They include the *Gibbons Catalogue* (Great Britain), *Michel* (Germany), *Yvert* and *Ceres* (France), *Bolaffi* (Italy), *Facit* (Scandinavia), *Netto* (Austria), and many others.

The role of the stamp catalogue is often misunderstood. Stamp catalogues are general guides to pricing. They attempt to reflect actual market prices, but do not determine them. Supply and demand determine market prices. Market prices—both retail and wholesale—often vary from catalogue prices, and often substantially. Stamp buying and selling prices are usually quoted in terms of discounts from catalogue, discounts that reflect actual price levels in the market. Figures published daily in the financial section of the newspaper do not determine the prices of stocks; they only reflect what has occurred in the market. Stamp catalogues perform the same function, except that they are usually published only once a year rather than daily. During the course of the year, the stamp market moves independently to its own rhythm. So the possibility of discrepancies between catalogue and market prices increases with the passing of time. And unlike stocks, stamps vary physically from one another (condition) and are therefore priced on an individual basis like gemstones. For these reasons, stamp catalogues are not absolute price authorities, only general guides.

Check retail advertisements in weekly philatelic periodicals for both individual stamps and country collections to get a feel for the real market. Retail offerings are usually priced at discounts from catalogue value. Discounts vary depending upon country, condition, etc. If you see stamps similar to yours offered at retail for one-half catalogue value, it is unrealistic to expect a dealer to pay half catalogue (full retail) for yours. In addition, philatelic weeklies contain lots of dealer buy ads. Many quote prices for specific items or specific countries. Finding nationally advertised buying prices, for even a few of your items, will give you a pretty good idea of the actual market value of your stamps.

Sellers often ask dealers, "At what discount from catalogue do you buy stamps?" The answer is that is no standard discount; it varies from item to item. The discount depends on the country, the condition, whether mint or used, classic or modern, and a number of other factors. Some stamps are worth full catalogue, while others are worth only a slight fraction of catalogue. For example, dealers pay only about five to ten percent of catalogue for faulty nineteenth century European stamps. By the same token, you can usually obtain these same stamps for a slight advance over what the dealer has paid, and he'll be glad be rid of them. Faulty stamps are not in demand. As a general rule, only the very best, most expensive stamps are worth a significant percentage of catalogue value.

The reason for the great variety of prices and percentages is that each stamp, especially expensive ones, is valued strictly according to its own merits. Browsing a stamp show, it is possible to find ten different copies of the same stamp with ten different prices. The vast range of prices is confusing to the newcomer, especially when he relies on the catalogue to be absolutely definitive. Just remember, catalogue prices are reference points; the market determines real prices. As a general rule, the greater the value of the stamp, the lower the markup. The markup on a $2,000 item may be as little as $100 to $300.

Common stamps, packet material, kiloware, approval short sets, and cancelled-to-order (CTO) stamps trade in bulk by the pound, by the hundred, by the thousand, or whatever. Their market value bears little relationship to catalogue value.

Stamps of industrialized nations tend to be worth more than stamps from third world countries. Nations with well-educated, affluent citizens have well-established collector bases and strong domestic stamp markets. Stamps from nations with strong domestic stamp markets hold their values best. By contrast, third world nations tend to have very thin domestic stamp markets. In addition, many third world nations pump out hundreds of colorful, and usually unnecessary, new issues per year in order to raise revenue. This practice tends to dilute the value and desirability of other stamps of these countries. Colorful, low-value, ultra-common CTO topicals are known in the trade as "wallpaper." They are used to make packets for beginners or for approvals. They are as ubiquitous as weeds and have little individual resale value. Dealers heap them in counter boxes or leave them in albums, pricing them at one or two cents each, regardless of their catalogue value.

Topical stamps for transient themes—such as World Refugee Year and even the American Bicentennial—are typically worth only a fraction of their new issue prices. Once the excitement of an event has passed, there is little demand in the secondary market for stamps commemorating it. The stamps are then as dead as yesterday's news. Ongoing topicals—such as flowers, space, dogs, etc.—tend to hold their value better.

Modern first day covers (FDCs) and mass-marketed special event covers—such as birthdays of the Presidents—are extremely abundant and with few exceptions, worth only a fraction of their original price in the secondary market. In contrast, hand-painted FDCs (those with cachet designs individually painted by hand) and pre-1940 FDCs, both of which are scarce, tend to hold their value better.

Most mint U.S. stamps issued after 1945 trade at a discount from face value when sold in bulk. This is hard for the newcomer to understand. The subject of discount postage is covered in greater detail later in this book. Suffice it to say that dealers pay anywhere from 70 to 90 percent of face value for most post-1945 mint stamps. The exact discount depends on the market at the time of sale. Full sheets usually bring more than singles, blocks, or scrap, because they are easier to handle and count.

Why is a three-cent stamp worth only 80 percent of face value although it catalogues 15 cents? Because most bulk discount postage sold to dealers ends up used on mail. The dealer buys at 80 percent and sells to the bulk mailer at 90 percent. Each makes ten percent for his trouble. Without the ten percent incentive, neither would have any reason to buy large quantities of old postage.

What about the three-cent stamp that actually retails for fifteen cents? The best analogy is "parts and labor": three cents parts and twelve cents labor. Even on those rare occasions when a three-cent stamp actually sells for full catalogue, there is little real profit—the exercise is simply too time and labor intensive.

One more word about minimum catalogue value. Every stamp has a minimum catalogue value, regardless of how common it is. Ordinary stamps—the kind you receive on your mail every day—catalogue fifteen cents each used, but rarely, if ever, is one actually purchased from a dealer. Regard the minimum catalogue value for ultra-common used stamps as a service charge to compensate a dealer for his time and trouble if he is actually called upon to provide an individual copy. The used stamp itself is basically worthless.

I once received a phone call from a wastepaper dealer on the East Coast who had access to empty envelopes from a utility company. He had accumulated a semi-trailer full of envelopes, stamps still attached, that he wanted to sell. He estimated that the trailer contained at least a million stamps, mostly common definitives. Using the then-current minimum catalogue value of five cents each, he arrived at a value of $50,000. He offered to sell the whole lot, including delivery, for $5,000. When I declined, he countered with an offer of $2,500. At that point, I told him I wasn't interested at any price. He laughed good humoredly and said he wasn't surprised. He thought five cents a stamp sounded too good to be true. After all, who would pay a nickel for something that could be had for nothing off incoming mail. Such realists are uncommon in the stamp business.

GIGO (garbage in, garbage out), the well-known computer axiom, is likewise applicable to stamp collections. Don't expect a beginner collection on which a few dollars were initially spent to suddenly be worth a lot of money, even decades later. Don't expect a collection formed from packets obtained at the five-and-dime to suddenly be worth hundreds or thousands of dollars. Valuable collections are typically formed over decades by methodical individuals who spend meaningful sums of money on better than average items.

One more point. Used albums, supplies, and the labor invested in mounting a collection have virtually no resale value.

In summary, each stamp is priced according to its merits, and generally, the more expensive the stamp, the less the markup. So many variables are involved in pricing that catalogues serve only as general guides, not absolutes. Check philatelic weeklies for buy and sell ads to get a feel for the market. Newcomers are hard-pressed to assimilate quickly all the complexities of the market. If you feel overwhelmed, consult a dealer. Ask questions. Dealers are good sources of up-to-date pricing information. Remember, the final arbiter of value is the market. An item is worth only as much as the best offer—no more.

VALUING A SPECIFIC PROPERTY

Experienced dealers are proficient at valuing collections speedily. Sellers, especially those with little knowledge of stamps, are constantly amazed by how little time it takes a professional to make an evaluation. Having struggled to make sense of paper varieties, watermarks, and perforations, the bewildered seller wonders how a dealer can skim through a collection and evaluate it accurately. There is no secret to valuing collections quickly and accurately; it's simply a matter of knowledge and experience. Experienced buyers have spent thousands and thousands of hours working with collections. They know the key stamps of the world intimately, including their current market values.

Knowledge and experience permit a dealer to use valuing shortcuts. The most common technique is to count the value of the keys of a country and then add a sum for the balance.

For example, the keys to a U.S. airmail collection are the first six stamps and the Zeppelin set. A collection lacking these two groups—and most collections do—is usually worth less than $100. Dealers check for those keys, then add in the balance. It's just that simple and takes only a minute or two. Another example: collections of mint U.S. commemorative stamps from about 1940 onward—the most commonly encountered type—typically have a value of less than a few hundred dollars. Dealers have no need to run an adding machine tape on this type collection. It takes only a moment to establish the degree of completeness and apply a dollar value according to known increments. Collections of mint U.S. commemorative singles issued between 1940-1960 are worth about $20; 1960-1969, about $10; 1970-1979, about $40; and 1980-1989, about $100, and so forth. It takes only another moment to add in high-value definitives, if any are present. Only the earlier, individually more valuable stamps are counted on a stamp-by-stamp basis. Plate block collections are figured in the same fashion. The idea is to arrive at an accurate value without wasting time.

United Nations collections are, likewise, easy to calculate. The first souvenir sheet (the 1955 tenth-anniversary issue) is the key to a U.N. collection. At this writing, dealer buy prices for it are around $70 to $80, depending on condition. It's the first thing a dealer checks for. If the collection contains it, he starts at $80 (or less depending on condition) and calculates the balance according to its degree of completeness. Collections of mint U.N. stamps from the years 1951-1959 have a face value of around $10; 1960-1969 about $15; 1970-1979 about $25; and 1980-1989 about $70; and so forth. Calculating a U.N. collection is a simple matter taking only a few moments. There's no mystery to it at all.

Each country has its keys and its common stamps. The same technique can be applied to all. Count the keys individually; add in the balance. The majority of stamps from most countries were issued after World War II, and of these, most have a comparatively low catalogue value that tends to be fairly constant from stamp to stamp. In fact, nine out of ten collections, regardless of the country, lack most keys and consist largely of these common stamps. The calculation of modern collections is really an exercise in bulk, i.e., 500 stamps at 20 cents (or whatever value is appropriate) equals $100, and so forth. Each dealer uses his own formula, but all are based on the same principle: value the keys individually; value the balance in bulk.

It is difficult for anyone not familiar with stamps to understand the degree of familiarity with them that the average dealer possesses. Remember, dealers look at the same stamps day-in and day-out; they know their values well. Sellers often misinterpret speed for careless or inattentive work; however just because an evaluation takes little time, does not mean it is inaccurate. It is not uncommon for different dealers to go quickly through the same multi-volume collection and come up with figures less than five percent apart, even on collections in the $10,000 to $20,000 range.

I've had more than one experience with individuals who could not understand how the task of valuing stamps could be accomplished so quickly. A telephone conversation with a particularly hard-headed individual stands out in my mind.

"I'm interested in selling my collection," the caller began. "But I want a careful evaluation, not one of those snap offers."

"Snap offers?" I repeated, not sure what he meant.

"Yeah, you know—flips through the albums in ten minutes and makes an offer. I don't want any of you dealers who think you can just take a quick look at the collection and make a snap offer. I'm just not interested in a snap offer."

"I take it you've had other offers?"

"Yeah, a while back. A couple of different guys came out, looked at the stamps, and made snap offers that didn't amount to much. They hardly spent any time at all on 'em, so I figured I'd just keep 'em. I'm not about to let 'em go to some snap-offer artist." His voice sounded cynical, arrogant, and confrontational. I knew right away that it would be a waste of time to look at this fellow's collection. He wouldn't be satisfied with the way I went about my evaluation. Judging by his comments about other offers, his collection probably contained low-grade material of which he had a very high opinion.

He had it fixed in his mind that the size of an offer was directly proportional to the amount of time spent looking at the stamps. He had generalized his own lack of knowledge about stamps to the dealers who looked at his collection. He assumed that since they didn't spend much time on it, they weren't doing a good job of valuing. Unfortunately, no amount of time spent looking at mediocre stamps will improve their value.

"Do you really want to know the true value of your stamps?" I asked, as if I might let him in on a big secret. "Do you really want to know how to tell if you're being taken?" Of course he did. Given his personality and attitude, which left little doubt that he regarded all dealers as charlatans, the information had to be irresistible. I sensed that he was one of those sour individuals who feel that the whole world is trying to take advantage of them. The line was silent for a long moment as, even then, he pondered the possibility of a catch.

"Sure," he eventually replied, guardedly.

"Your stamps are worth whatever you can get for them. No more, no less. Get three offers, or five, or five hundred—however many makes you happy. When you're satisfied that you've gotten enough opinions, take the highest one. That's what your stamps are worth. The amount of time a dealer spends valuing your collection is not important; the only important fact is what you can get for it."

"I'm still not taking any snap offers," he retorted defiantly. "If you're interested in making a legitimate offer, come on out."

"No thanks," I replied. "You seem to be more interested in how someone goes about making an offer than what the offer is. Chances are you'd think that my offer was a snap offer if I didn't spend as much time paging through your collection as you thought I should. There are plenty of other dealers around. Perhaps one of them will be interested."

His attitude was bound to offend just about any dealer he called. He was never going to find one who give him as much as he thought his stamps were worth.

Nor is his attitude isolated. On another occasion, I received a call from a man who said that his collection was too massive to bring to the office, so I went to him.

J.B., a newly hired assistant eager to learn the buying end of the stamp business, accompanied me. It was his first day on the job, and on the way out, I explained some of the techniques of stamp buying.

The seller lived in a run-down mobile home on the outskirts of Denver. The interior was cramped and cluttered; it reminded me of an unmade bed. The collection—actually it was more of an accumulation—was housed in several large, old, green metal cabinets, each containing a multitude of small drawers. Each drawer was packed with hundreds of glassine envelopes into which stamps had been sorted. After a few pleasantries, I began. As I pulled out the first drawer, our host leaned forward. Like a bird perched on fencepost, he turned his head turned ever so slightly, his unblinking eye scrutinizing my every move. I don't recall the man's name, but to this day I remember him as "Hawkeye."

It is my custom to first go through a large property quickly to get a general idea of its scope, then review it again more carefully to arrive at a final figure. A preliminary scan enables me to identify important sections and better budget my time for the second, more careful inspection. This technique is especially useful on the road, when one must keep a tight appointment schedule. After all, the idea is to arrive at the best, most competitive offer in the time available.

The first handful of glassines was disappointing: German States, every stamp faulty, worth perhaps five percent of catalogue at best. Sound top-quality classics are very scarce; defective copies are plentiful. Only sound German States—which are seldom encountered—are worth anywhere near catalogue value. Faulty German States sell for deep discounts precisely because they are so plentiful and difficult to sell; condition-conscious collectors shun them. Dealers are reluctant to buy collections whose primary value arises from defective early stamps with high catalogue prices, let alone argue about what percent of catalogue they're worth.

I checked the rest of the first file drawer quickly, riffling through the glassines a handful at a time. The stamps were all used, mostly common issues that hopscotched unevenly over the years. Key stamps, when present, were damaged. By the end of the first drawer, I had a strong feeling that quantity, rather than quality, would be the rule. The next few drawers confirmed my suspicion. Hawkeye's accumulation was a low-budget endeavor composed of tens of thousands of stamps soaked off countless pounds of kiloware and dutifully organized into thousands of glassine envelopes. It was packet material, pure and simple, with a few high-catalogue clunkers scattered here and there to break up the monotony.

I worked rapidly but Hawkeye was not impressed by my speed.
"You're not looking at each stamp," he said, frowning. "How are
you going to know how much the collection's worth if you don't
price each envelope?"

"I'm just getting a general idea of what you've got here. So far
I've seen only common, used stamps—the kind that go into
packets. Is the entire collection like this?" I asked, hoping, but not
really expecting, to find a section of mint stamps.

Experienced stamp dealers acquire detective skills that enable
them to quickly form opinions about collections from clues in both
the stamps and the owners. Collectors are creatures of habit. Each
has specific acquiring and spending habits. A collector may not be
aware of his pattern, but it's readily apparent to the dealer. The
best items in a given collection tend to hover near a certain
maximum figure. If the figure is $25, for example, stamps worth
more than that will seldom be encountered. The figure may be 25
cents a stamp, $10 a stamp, $100 a stamp, or any number.

Further, it is quickly apparent whether an individual is condition
conscious or tolerates damaged stamps. If the first few keys are
flawless, then generally the rest of the collection will be of high
quality. If the first few keys are faulty, the collector is more cost
conscious than quality conscious, and faults can be expected
throughout the collection. Once the general nature of a collection
reveals itself, the pattern rarely digresses. An experienced dealer
can tell right away just how good a collection is. And in this case,
the evidence pointed to low-quality, low-priced stamps.

"There may be a few mint stamps here and there," Hawkeye
said. "But mostly they're used. What difference does it make
anyway?" His voice rose. "There's a lot of stamps here. They
add up to a lot of money—but you're not counting every one.
How can you get an accurate idea of the exact value of the
collection? You skipped right over the German States. They
catalogue a bundle."

"But they're all faulty," I replied, thumbing through glassines as
I spoke. "Some have pieces missing. They're of nominal value at
best. The other stamps are all used—common—packet material.
The kind you figure based on bulk, not stamp by stamp."

"There's no use going any further," he said peremptorily. "If
you're not going count each stamp, I don't see how you're going
to be able to make a reasonable offer." Then he said, "You're just

like the others—but that's *not* how I'm going to do business. I want every stamp counted, and I expect to be paid accordingly. If you're not going to do the job right, there's no use going any further."

"You're right," I replied, returning stamp tongs and pad to my attaché case. "No use wasting my time or yours." I snapped the case shut and rose. Other dealers had been there before me, and Hawkeye had been dissatisfied with the way they had gone about making their offers.

He assumed that once he had organized his stamps in glassines, a dealer would calculate their catalogue values stamp by stamp, total the figures, and make an offer—which he almost certainly thought would be a considerable sum. Unfortunately, the stamps were so common that individual catalogue values were irrelevant. I wondered why he hadn't catalogued the stamps himself since he had gone to the trouble of organizing them into glassines.

"You damn stamp dealers are all alike," he snarled viciously as I rose to leave. Anger and frustration boiled up and rippled across his face. He made no attempt to hide his emotions.

"Let's go," I said to J.B., who had been watching wide-eyed. I marched full-speed, straight ahead, out the front door and to the car. J.B. was at my heels. A raging Hawkeye hurled epithets from his front doorway as we left. His words were indistinct; his fury was not.

"Boy, I hope they're not all like that," J.B. said after we were in the car.

"They're not, believe me," I replied, chuckling inwardly at J.B.'s unusual introduction to the stamp business. "Difficult personalities go with the territory. But you can't let them bother you. Fortunately, most people are reasonable and pleasant to deal with."

In summary, give a dealer credit for knowing his field. He doesn't need to refer to the catalogue page by page in order to value a collection. In fact, you might be wary of someone who finds it necessary to do that; he certainly can't be very knowledgeable. After all, how much confidence would you have in a surgeon who found it necessary to constantly refer to a medical text while performing surgery on you?

ALL THAT GLITTERS

This chapter is directed to those new to the field of stamps. You have acquired a collection: perhaps a bequest, a gift, or a purchase made at a garage sale or flea market. In any event, you page through it mystified and at the same time intrigued. You have heard that stamps are valuable, and you wonder what treasures lie waiting to be discovered in the collection at hand.

First, you refer to a stamp catalogue and try to understand the meaning of the listings that fill page after page. Tantalizingly you find one of your stamps illustrated, but several varieties exist. Is yours the common five-cent variety or the $10,000 rarity? You're not sure; the catalogue descriptions are confusing. What is meant by perf 10? By rotary press? And how do you detect a watermark?

Chances are the catalogue is mystifying because you haven't read the introduction carefully. You'd be surprised how many people don't. It's a common mistake. The catalogue offers a wealth of information. Unfortunately, without a thorough reading of the introduction, it's difficult to utilize the listings properly. Be sure to read catalogue introductions carefully, especially if you have no previous experience with stamps. You'll avoid a lot of confusion later.

Another common mistake made by those unfamiliar with stamps and stamp catalogues is to automatically assume, when a question of variety arises, that they have the scarce variety. I've recieved hundreds of calls over the years from people who claim that their album contains not only one but numerous examples of the rarest varieties, when in fact, they have the most common ones.

Once I received a call from an excited individual who had purchased a box of viewcards at a garage sale. He joyfully related to me how every single card (about 500 in all) was franked with the rare, one-cent perforated 11, rotary-press waste variety of the 1922 definitive series, a stamp that catalogues $32,500 at this writing. He was sure he had millions of dollars worth of stamps. He could barely contain his excitement. I knew better. I explained that the stamp was so rare that only about a dozen copies had ever been documented. The viewcards in his box had been mailed from numerous locations over a wide period of time. The rare variety is known to have been used in only a couple of cities and only for a brief time. It was impossible for every card in the box to contain the rarity. But no amount of explaining would him dissuade from his belief. Finally, I advised him to seek out a dealer whose bank account might contain the millions necessary to purchase his newfound treasure as mine was not sufficient to acquire it.

The rare one-cent perforated 11 rotary-press waste variety of the 1922 definitive series is just one example of a stamp commonly misidentified. Its design, featuring a portrait of Benjamin Franklin, exists on common varieties and rarities alike. The most commonly encountered varieties are the flat plate versions, perforated either 11 (when perforations are of the same gauge on all sides, they are referred to by a single numeral—such as 11—rather than 11 x 11) or perforated 10, and the rotary press version perforated 11 x 10½. Flat plate and rotary printings differ slightly in dimension, by a fraction of a millimeter. The common varieties are abundant, especially used; they did routine postal duty for more than a decade and a half.

However, the exact same design exists on a couple of rarities. They are the rotary-press printed sheet stamps perforated 11 (instead of the normal 11 x 10½) and coil waste stamps perforated on all four sides (instead of being perforated on only two sides and made into coil stamps). The Bureau of Engraving and Printing salvaged small end-portions of these rotary-press runs and perforated them 11 rather than waste them, hence their name "waste varieties." Another rotary-press waste variety, scarce but by no means rare, exists perforated 11 x 10. The valuable rotary-press waste varieties vary in dimension from the flat plate printings, and vary in perforation from subsequent rotary-press sheet printings, their common counterparts. Even a novice can detect these differences with a perforation gauge and millimeter rule. So take time to read the introduction to the catalogue carefully so that you can identify the varieties before jumping to conclusions.

At this writing, catalogue price for used examples of the two most common varieties of the one-cent Franklin definitive of the 1922 series is fifteen cents each. The somewhat scarcer rotary press, perforated 10 variety catalogues 65 cents used. In contrast, catalogue values for used examples of the two rare varieties are $4,750 and $32,500 respectively. The third scarce variety catalogues $140 used.

Most catalogues assign an identifying number (as distinct from a catalogue number) to each stamp design irrespective of perforation or other subtle varieties. Each of these varieties (varieties in perforation, watermark, etc.) is assigned its own catalogue number. It is, therefore, possible for several stamps of the same basic design to have different catalogue numbers (and prices) because they differ in subtle ways. The catalogue number usually appears first (to the left) in a listing with the identifying number located to it's immediate right. If you don't know better, it's easy to run down a catalogue page, spot a stamp worth $32,500 whose basic design is identical to one you have, and conclude that it is a rarity—unaware that half a dozen cheap varieties with the same design exist.

Many issues exist in both common and rare forms. The two-cent Harding memorial issue of 1923 exists in four varieties. The three common varieties range in price from 15 cents to $4.25 for used examples. The rare variety catalogues $15,000 at this writing. I have examined thousands of two-cent Harding memorials over the years and never once found the rare variety.

Nineteenth century issues are especially confusing to the uninitiated, who must contend with grills, paper varieties, reissues, and secret marks. In many cases, only the practiced eye can easily discern the differences. The range in catalogue values is enormous: from less than a dollar to tens of thousands of dollars, depending on variety. The Washington-Franklin series of 1908-1921, too, is a briar-patch of varieties. Again, read the introduction carefully before jumping to conclusions.

Fakes can also be a problem. Fakes of certain stamps are very common. The imperforate variety of the five-cent definitive of the 1902-1903 series is a good example. It's a simple matter to trim the perforations off a large-margined, used copy of the perforated variety (catalogue value $1.50), thus transforming it into the rarer imperforate variety (catalogue value $425). Imperforate stamps should be collected in pairs to confirm their genuineness. Imperforate single copies are salable only if expertized—more about that later. So don't get too excited if you find a used single of the imperforate five-cent definitive of 1902-1903 series in the old album you've just acquired; it's almost certainly a fake.

Expensive coil stamps are also frequently faked by trimming perforations off two sides of their inexpensive, fully perforated counterparts. And just because an album is 50 years old means nothing. Stamp faking is nothing new; fakers have been hard at work since Day One.

If you think you've come across a rare type, have a stamp dealer check it. It won't do any good to inquire by phone. He'll need to see it in order to identify it. Chances are that he won't charge to look at one or two stamps, but if you want a whole album checked, be ready to pay an appraisal fee. Also, bear in mind that the odds of discovering a real rarity are very, very slim. Don't be too surprised when your album full of potential treasures turns out to be common stamps.

If you do find a rare variety or disagree with the dealer's opinion, you can submit your stamp to an expertizing body such as the Philatelic Foundation or the American Philatelic Expertizing Service for a certificate of authenticity. These nonprofit organizations issue certificates that are widely accepted in the trade as proof-positive of genuineness. Expertizing fees are usually based on a small percentage of catalogue value. The investment in expertizing is modest compared to the value it adds to a stamp certified genuine. A minimum fee applies to stamps that turn out to be common varieties with low catalogue values. Addresses of expertizing organizations are listed in the Appendix.

In summary, don't automatically assume that you have the rarest variety. Read the catalogue carefully—especially the introduction—and check your stamps thoroughly before running to your local stamp dealer with the wonderful news that you have an album full of rarities. Just remember: "All that glitters is not gold."

APPRAISAL AND OFFER

The terms *appraisal* and *offer* are often confused. An appraisal is a valuation by an expert and is not necessarily an offer to buy. Stamps are appraised for a variety of reasons: insurance (typically figured at replacement cost), estates (typically figured at market value), legal settlements (divorces, judgments, etc.), and, of course, outright sale. Replacement value is the amount one would expect to spend buying at retail; market value is the amount one would expect to receive selling to a dealer. In most cases, an appraisal is a formal, written evaluation for which the owner pays a fee.

An offer to buy is not an appraisal. An offer is the amount a buyer is willing to pay for a property. An offer may be the result of hours of evaluation or just a few minutes—however long it takes the dealer to determine how much he is willing to pay. Dealers make offers based on their individual circumstances and needs. Therefore, an offer may be close to appraised value or it may not be. It depends on the market, and the opinion and the circumstances of a buyer on a given day. There is usually no fee for making an offer.

APPRAISAL
If you are unfamiliar with stamps or the stamp market, it may be wise to have an appraisal made before you solicit offers, especially if your collection is large or potentially valuable. Appraisal fees are usually based on either an hourly rate ($25 per hour or more) or a percentage of the value (typically starting at 2½ percent and dropping as the dollar value of the collection rises). On very large properties, fees are negotiable. For example, one

might expect to pay $250 (2½ percent) for appraisal of a $10,000 collection, yet only pay $5,000 (1 percent) for appraisal of a $500,000 collection. A minimum fee of $25 to $100 usually applies regardless of the value. Most dealers will refund their appraisal fee if they end up buying the collection. Even if you're not in the market to sell, there are other good reasons for having an appraisal made. One is to document value in case you ever need to make an insurance claim. Another is to determine the merits of insurance versus safe deposit storage.

On numerous occasions I have been invited to view "valuable" collections stored in safe deposit boxes, only to find dozens and dozens of albums of moderately-priced stamps. In many cases, safe deposit fees amounted to more than the stamps were worth.

A few years back, I made an appraisal for a man who had inherited a voluminous collection. He knew little about stamps. We met in the safe deposit area of his bank. It took the man and a bank attendant three trips to the vault with a cart to retrieve all the albums and boxes. We chatted as I looked through the collection. He told me it cost nearly $500 per year for safe deposit storage, that he'd spent more than $3,000 since inheriting the collection. The collection contained no stamps of significant individual value, just a great number of moderately priced stamps. The entire collections was worth about $4,500. I advised that it would be more economical to keep the collection at home and insure it. If left in the bank three more years, the cumulative expenditure for box rental fees would equal the entire value of the collection, and there seemed little likelihood that future appreciation would be enough to offset the annual cost of storage. This situation is not uncommon. Many people waste money on bank storage for stamps that could be more economically insured.

Remember, the vast majority of stamps in any collection are of moderate value. The expense of safe deposit storage makes sense only for very valuable stamps, such as Columbians and Zeppelins, which take up little space. For these, safe deposit box storage is more economical than insurance. Stamp insurance—such as that available through the American Philatelic Society (APS)—is much more cost effective for protecting bulky, moderately-priced collections. Tip: APS stamp insurance can usually be purchased for fraction of the cost of a collectibles rider to a conventional homeowner's policy.

Always have an appraisal done by a professional. Don't rely on the fellow down the street, who is rumored to be a stamp collector, for a realistic idea of value. It's not that he's not honest or trustworthy, it's just that he won't have the same intimate working knowledge of the stamp market and up-to-the-minute values that the professional has. Amateurs tend to grossly over-estimate market values. An unrealistic estimate only makes the unknowledgeable seller's task more difficult. When informed by a dealer of the real value of his stamps, which often varies greatly from the amateur opinion, the seller remains skeptical, and rightly so. He doesn't know who to believe. Remember, the opinion of an amateur is not a cash offer; it's a hypothetical opinion. Rarely, if ever, is it possible to find a live buyer who will pay an amateur appraiser's price.

Consider the case of the frustrated individual who was told by a friend of the family that the stamps he had inherited were worth $2,500. Unfortunately, the friend had been away from the hobby for a number of years. The heir, stamps in hand, proceeded to the nearest dealer to cash them in. The dealer offered $700. He shopped half a dozen more dealers. The best cash offer was $750. He wanted to know why he couldn't get full value—$2,500. The dealers were, in fact, quite willing to pay full value; the problem was that *real* full value was only $750, not $2,500. The well-meaning family friend was completely out of touch with the market.

The value of any commodity is that which the market will pay for it. Half a dozen offers in the same price range are more than enough to establish fair market value. Our frustrated collector friend could have gotten any number of additional offers, and the story would have been the same—they would have been right around $750. He could have saved himself a lot trouble by getting a professional opinion in the first place. A market-value appraisal would have given him an idea of what he could reasonably expect to get for his collection.

Don't expect to get an informed opinion of stamp values from an antique dealer, an autograph dealer, an art dealer, or even a coin dealer. They may be quite knowledgeable in their own fields but not as knowledgeable about stamps as a stamp dealer. For the best advice about stamps, contact a professional who buys and sells stamps every day and knows market values. When you require reliable medical or legal information, you consult a professional. Stamps are no different. When you want reliable information, consult a professional. If you know little about stamps, an appraisal is money well spent.

OFFER

An offer is a dealer's spot cash price. An offer is based on a variety of factors including a dealer's circumstances and his attitude toward the stamps. Offers can vary, although for routine stamps, such as general U.S. collections, they tend to be similar.

Understand that an offer reflects a dealer's attitude toward your specific stamps and his specific needs. Remember, he's buying your stamps for resale, not because their value is etched in stone somewhere.

There are many kinds of stamp dealers: general dealers, specialists, large dealers, small dealers, etc. The dealer with immediate need for your stamps will make the best offer. A dealer specializing in packets is not likely to be the best market for a rare inverted Jenny. Likewise, the upscale dealer specializing in scarce high-priced stamps is not likely to be interested in acquiring 100,000 common commemoratives soaked off paper. A western dealer is not likely to prize a collection of New York postal history as much as an eastern dealer. A dealer specializing in Germany is not likely to have any interest in Peruvian stamps. And so on.

And there are other factors. A small dealer may be intimidated by a large, valuable holding. He may be uncomfortable investing a large portion of his capital in it. On the other hand, he may be much more eager to buy a collection of moderately priced stamps than a large dealer who already has a back room full of them. Even a large dealer may be unfamiliar with narrowly specialized material, such as newly discovered error stamps. He may have no clientele for it or be unsure of the market for it.

The market is full of variables. A low offer usually indicates that, for whatever reason, a dealer really isn't eager to buy your collection. He may be new to the business, inexperienced, and unsure of values. He may be overstocked with what you have for sale. He may be short of cash and simply not able to offer more. He may be approaching retirement and not eager to acquire more inventory. Numerous factors influence a dealer's offer, none of which may relate to the objective value of your stamps.

Some collections are so esoteric that few dealers have any notion of their value. A friend of mine collects town postmarks of Katanga, the short-lived rebel state that controlled part of the Belgian Congo after its independence in 1960. The material is very scarce, no question about it. In the entire world, there are perhaps a dozen collectors of Katanga town cancels, a mere handful who can appreciate the material's scarcity.

I have often thought that regardless of where the collection was brought to market, it would attract only low offers, if any at all. Katanga town cancels are simply too esoteric. Very few dealers have any knowledge of or experience with them. The average dealer has no market for them and therefore no way to value them. When considering how much to offer for such a collection, these questions would run through his mind: "How long would I have to wait for the right customer to come along?" "How much would he be willing to pay?" "How much effort and expense would be entailed in finding that right customer?" "How long would the collection sit on the shelf?" "Indeed, how much should I risk to acquire such an esoteric property?" And the answer is likely to be "Not much."

It all comes down to potential profit; risk versus reward. In the final analysis, a dealer's offer will be a price at which he feels comfortable; one that balances risk and reward.

Bear in mind that discrepancies in offers are usually the result of honest differences in how a collection is perceived. The dealer who runs a small shop, who has no market for high-powered classics, isn't necessarily trying to cheat you because his offer is low. More than likely he's unfamiliar with the material, doesn't have a market for it, and is uncomfortable writing a large check to acquire it. He's simply the wrong dealer for it. Remember, the dealer with immediate need for your stamps will make the best offer.

To be prudent, get several offers. My experience is that two or three are sufficient. Usually by the third offer, a seller becomes aware of just how much his stamps are really worth. There are exceptions, however, such as error stamps. Because errors are so specialized, a complete chapter has been devoted to selling them.

Some dealers refuse to make offers for free. Usually, for a fee, they will make an appraisal backed by cash—in effect, an offer. The fee is waived or refunded if they subsequently buy the collection. Or they will request that the seller name his asking price, a figure the seller is usually reluctant to reveal (more about that in the chapter "Getting to Yes"). The reason many dealers are reluctant to make free offers is that all too often the seller accepts the very next offer at a slight advance over theirs. Dealer's don't want to do all the work with no opportunity to benefit.

Herman Herst Jr., noted dealer and philatelic author, had a notice posted in his store to that effect: "I never make offers. Were I to put the work in that is necessary to figure a collection, it would be a simple matter for the prospective seller to take my offer to my neighbor and induce him to raise it, and then go to his neighbor and induce him to raise that. The last man in the chain, who had done no work in figuring it, would thus be the gainer for all the work that had been done by his predecessors. When I sell stamps, I don't ask for offers, but price all my own merchandise. The fairest method for anyone wanting to do business with me is to price his stamps, too."

You may be wondering what good an appraisal is if offers can vary. Though offers *can* vary substantially, it doesn't mean they will. It has been my experience that most offers are in the same ballpark. Likewise, *most* dealers are perfectly steady and reliable. The factors that can affect a dealer's buying decisions are mentioned only to provide a complete picture of the market. Extreme cases tend to be the exception rather than the rule. The fact is that appraisals are usually on target, and most dealers will be in the market to buy at prices close to a market appraisal, assuming the appraisal is recent.

SELLING BY MAIL OR PHONE

There are numerous situations in which dealing by phone or mail make sense. You may live in a remote area. You may have a sizable collection beyond the reach of a small local dealer. You may wish to take advantage of a big city market. You may have stamps of interest to a specialist located far away. Or you may have seen an advertisement to buy from a dealer in a distant city. Whatever the case, dealing by phone or mail gives you access to every dealer in the nation.

Many, especially those unfamiliar with stamps, are reluctant to do business by phone or mail. You shouldn't worry so long as you deal with an established, reliable dealer. Again, if in doubt, ask for references, length of time in business, and professional credentials such as ASDA membership.

THE INITIAL CONTACT

Before you call or write, organize facts about your collection so that you can provide meaningful information to the dealer you contact. Don't assume that a dealer will be interested just because you announce that you have stamps for sale. He'll need specific information about your collection before he can decide whether to travel to your location, ask you to ship it for an offer, or give you some other advice. Be prepared to furnish specific details. Stamp dealers receive so many calls about collections—most of which are relatively insignificant—that they tend to be very selective about those they choose to follow up. It makes no sense for a dealer to put a prospective seller to the expense of shipping an unwanted collection and himself to the trouble of returning it, if it can be avoided. Information along the following lines will enable a stamp dealer to form a pretty good picture of your collection. **Size.** How large is the collection? Try to be specific, e.g. the collection consists of U.S. stamps in five volumes, three stockbooks, and several hundred plate blocks organized in glassines; or the collection consists of general foreign in 40 partially filled volumes; or the collection consists of 2,000 first day covers from the period 1942-to-date; or the collection consists of six large cartons containing tens of thousands of new issues in glassines organized chronologically, spanning the years 1956 to 1984; or it consists of one small, thin album containing both U.S. and foreign. Don't give meaningless information such as "I've got gobs and gobs of stamps—I just don't know how to begin to tell you what's here." I know it sounds ridiculous, but you'd be amazed at the number of callers who've wanted me to fly to see their stamps based on just that sort of description.

Scope. Describe the range and extent of the collection. Again, try to be specific, e.g., United States single stamps, U.S. plate blocks, British Commonwealth, general foreign (i.e. stamps of all nations), specialized foreign (albums devoted to stamps of a single nation only—such as Germany, France or Canada), topical stamps (flowers, dogs, trains, space, music, etc.), first day covers, postal history, and so forth. The collection may not be mounted in albums; it may be housed in boxes, bags, or envelopes and appear disorganized. Nevertheless, attempt to describe it as accurately as possible. In the case of collections of worldwide stamps, try to describe the era (the span of years the covered by the collection) and the nations with the greatest concentration of stamps. And note whether sets tend to be complete or short (short sets contain only lower denominations, which are not worth much). Be sure to mention key stamps of significant value such as the U.S. Zeppelin set, if possible. The more specific the information, the more helpful it is.

Albums. Frequently, you will be asked what brand or name appears on your albums. Album names provide useful clues about how advanced and, therefore, how valuable a collection might be. Inexpensive, beginner's worldwide stamp albums contain spaces for only the most common stamps; even when chock-full, they are worth relatively little. On the other hand, a multi-volume collection housed in hingeless albums, which are expensive, indicates a potentially valuable collection.

Mint or used. Note whether the stamps are mint (uncancelled) or used (cancelled). If the collection contains a combination, estimate the proportion; 20 percent mint/80 percent used, 50 percent mint/50 percent used, or whatever. As a general rule, mint stamps are more desirable than used, however there are exceptions. Avoid the term "uncirculated"; it is a coin collector's term that has no meaning in philately.

Age. Note the range of years covered in each section of the collection. This is especially significant for U.S. collections and specialized foreign collections. For example, U.S. stamps, mostly 1890 to present—with a few prior to 1890; plate blocks from about 1935 to present; or U.N. singles from 1951 to 1970; or several volumes of general foreign with mostly post-1945 mint stamps. Remember, the more information you provide, the better.

Condition. Describe the general appearance and condition of the collection. Even those with no previous stamp experience can get a pretty good idea of a collection's general condition. In general terms, make note of the following: Are mint stamps hinged or in mounts? Are stamps carefully mounted or just jumbled together haphazardly? Are they fresh and attractive? Do they contain faults: tears, thins, pieces missing, etc.? Was completeness attempted or are spaces filled in random fashion? Does it appear that serious time, effort, and money went into the collection?

You don't have to be an expert to get a general impression of condition. A well-manicured yard is easy to recognize; it looks a lot different than a weed-infested, poorly cared for property. The same applies to stamps.

A reminder: Don't tamper with stamps in an attempt to improve their appearance. You'll do more harm than good. Don't remove stamps from envelopes. Don't attempt to clean dirty stamps or envelopes. Don't attempt to pull up stuck down stamps. Leave everything intact as you found it.

Value. Give the catalogue value, if known. Catalogue value is an instant point of reference. Be sure to state the catalogue and edition used because catalogue prices vary, both up and down, from year to year. An inventory is also very useful but not essential. Any other information—such as receipts for new issues, the face value of a mint sheet accumulation, or an appraisal—is also useful.

However, don't worry if you don't have an inventory, catalogue value, etc.; it is not imperative. A dealer can usually get a pretty good feel for your collection from the other facts you have given.

Remember, the information you provide determines how the dealer will react to your phone call. He'll base his decision about whether to travel to see your stamps, invite you to ship them, or offer some other advice based on this preliminary information. Don't risk failing to interest the best possible buyer by not providing enough information to justify his attention. First impressions are important.

A telephone call or letter is only the first step. Next comes actual inspection of the stamps. No dealer will make an offer without first seeing your stamps. If the collection is large enough, he may be willing to travel to your home. If not, he may suggest that you ship it to him for evaluation.

When making an inquiry by mail, send an inventory if you have one. If not, send the most detailed description possible. The purpose of the inventory or description is to establish interest. Be sure to include your telephone number or numbers (indicate home or work and best time to call). Busy dealers prefer to call rather than write. Remember, you won't get an offer based on an inventory or description alone; the dealer will have to see the stamps first. If sending inquiries to multiple dealers, don't expect to hear from every one. Large dealers, especially those who get great numbers of mail inquiries, often do not respond unless they have definite interest in a collection or unless the sender has included a self-addressed, stamped envelope (SASE).

Don't send samples of stamps from your collection with a mail inquiry. It's just not possible to generalize the value of a collection from a sample. A dealer needs to see the whole collection in order to get an idea of its value.

Dealers travel to buy only collections large enough to justify the expense. Typically, the minimum net value must be in the $5,000 to $10,000 range. Travel is covered in more detail in the next chapter.

SHIPPING STAMPS

Often, shipping is the most expedient way to bring buyer and seller together. Many sellers—especially those unfamiliar with the hobby—have reservations about sending their stamps through the mail to someone they have never met and know little about. Selling by mail is safe if you deal with a reliable, established dealer. Ask for general and bank references, number of years in business, and professional credentials such as ASDA membership. There are plenty of reliable dealers around, so you should have no trouble finding one who can serve your needs. Depending on the kind of stamps you have, reluctance to use the mails could severely limit your potential.

Before shipping your stamps, get a commitment about when you may expect payment if a price is agreed upon. Immediate payment on acceptance of an offer is standard. Avoid offers of installment payments.

It is also wise to agree in advance about who will pay the cost of returning the shipment in the event an offer is unacceptable. Many dealers will pay return shipping, especially if your material sounds interesting to them. Others require senders to pay return shipping, especially where no appraisal fee is involved. The policy varies from dealer to dealer, so clarify the terms before you ship.

Pack your stamps securely and send them by registered mail. For a modest fee, you can insure registered mail up to $25,000 per parcel. It's the safest way to ship stamps. Be sure to use paper tape on registered mail. The U.S. Postal Service will not accept registered parcels sealed with plastic tapes, including reinforced fiber tapes. This because they rubber stamp all the taped seams to evidence that the package has not been tampered with, something they don't do on regular parcel post (where us of plastic tape is okay). Don't use certified mail; it carries no insurance coverage.

Some individuals ship by United Parcel Service (UPS) because it is less expensive. Normally, UPS will not accept high dollar shipments, citing a policy excluding parcels of "extraordinary value." To circumvent this rule, some shippers lie about the contents, apparently unaware that misrepresentation is grounds for disallowing a claim in the event a shipment is lost or stolen.

In summary, dealing by phone or mail gives you access to every dealer in the nation. Remember, first impressions are important. Organize information about your collection so that you can communicate meaningful details to those you contact. The more specifics, the better. Deal with established, reliable dealers. Always have an understanding of the terms before you ship your stamps. Always ship by registered mail to protect yourself.

HAVE CHECK, WILL TRAVEL

Many stamp dealers will travel to buy a collection if it appears to justify the expense of the trip.   Before a dealer makes a commitment to travel (especially when airfare, auto rental, etc., are involved), he will want to be sure that the size of the collection justifies the trip *and* that he has a very good chance of making a deal.   The question I ask sellers who want me to fly to their location is: "Are you prepared to do business on the spot if my offer is reasonable?"   If the answer is yes, I go.   If the seller is not yet prepared to act decisively, I won't go—unless the seller is willing to reimburse my travel expenses.

Dealers ask a lot of questions before committing to travel.   The questions aren't intended to pin you down or to find out how cheaply you'll sell, but rather to establish the magnitude of the collection and whether you're ready to do business.

The following episode illustrates how the decision to travel is reached.   I received a call from a man in a small rural town in Pennsylvania about selling his late father's U.S. stamp collection.   I'll call him Mr. Whitaker.   According to Mr. Whitaker, the collection was loaded with key stamps.   He had gotten an offer from the only dealer in his area, the owner of a small shop in a nearby town, but Mr. Whitaker felt that he should have another opinion.   He wanted to know if I would fly from Colorado to see his collection.

"I'll fly if the collection's worth at least $5,000 net," I advised.

"Oh, it's worth at least that much based on the other offer I've had."

"Also, I cannot afford to make a trip unless you *are* serious about selling."

At that point, he became hesitant. He didn't want to commit to a sale before he knew how much offer was. I, too, was hesitant because my money—to the tune of several hundred dollars—would be on the line for airfare, car rental, and lodging. I didn't press the point, but mentioned it only for the sake of being straightforward about the expense involved and about my expectations.

"The collection is comprehensive," he said. "It contains a lot of expensive stamps."

I asked him to send photocopies so that I could confirm its size and scope. When they arrived, I was impressed. The collection appeared to be every bit as nice as he'd described.

I called him immediately. "I'd like to see the collection," I said. "I'm sure my offer will be well above $5,000 based on what I've seen . . . assuming there are no surprises. Stamps stuck down to pages, water damaged, that kind of thing."

He assured me that the stamps were in good shape. Dealers stress the issue of condition because there is a tendency among sellers to be imprecise about it. No one wants to waste airfare to see valuable stamps stuck down (as opposed to being correctly hinged) to album pages or otherwise impaired. Questions asked early on avoid later misunderstandings.

"I'll make the trip if you're serious about selling," I reiterated.

"I can't guarantee that I'll take your offer before I've heard it," he responded.

"I understand. I just want to be sure that if I make a reasonable offer you'll be ready to do business. I'm sure you can appreciate my position. You said that you've had another offer. If you plan to get any other offers, please do so before I go to the expense of flying out. I won't be able to make two trips in the event you want to think over my offer. I want to be sure that you're ready to do business if I make a fair offer."

"Can you give me a figure?" he asked.

"Not without seeing the stamps first. If I quote a strong figure, and it turns out that the stamps have problems that I couldn't detect from the photocopies, the actual figure will be lower, and you'll be upset. On the other hand, if I quote a low figure to take into account the worst possible case, you'll assume that I'm not competitive. It's a no-win situation."

"Can't you give me some idea?" he persisted.

"Well, based on what I've seen, probably in the $15,000 to $20,000 range. Remember, the figure could be higher or lower

depending upon condition. Would you do business in the $15,000
to $20,000 range?"
"Yes."
"And we can close a deal right away if everything checks out?"
"Yes."
"Fine, I'll be out," I said.
I flew out the following week. We met at his bank. I looked
the collection over and offered $19,000. He accepted and we
closed the deal on the spot.
One more point relating to offers. After we had closed the deal,
Mr. Whitaker told me that my offer was substantially higher than
the local dealer's. Was the local dealer trying to cheat him? I
don't think so. More likely he was a small town fellow who was
not used to seeing expensive stamps. The size of the collection
probably intimidated him, and his offer reflected that. He chose to
play it safe. He offered what his experience allowed him to feel
comfortable risking. He made an offer knowing, as all dealers
know or should know, that if it does not stand up to competition,
the collection will be lost to someone else.

Stamp dealers go on so many wild-goose chases that they soon
become very selective about which collections they follow up.
This is especially true when serious travel is involved. In the
previous chapter I stressed the importance of giving the best
telephone description possible. The decision to travel, to invite the
seller to ship, or to offer some other advice is based on those
all-important first few minutes of conversation. In some cases,
caution and selectivity must be weighed against the possibility that
an owner is simply unable to give a precise or meaningful
description.
A few years ago I received a call from a woman in Phoenix,
whom I'll call Mrs. Nelson. She owned a large collection and
wanted to know if I would fly to Phoenix to buy it. The
conversation was typical; the result was not. It went something
like this.
"How large is your collection?" I asked.
"Hundreds of thousands of stamps," she replied. I immediately
visualized pounds and pounds of inexpensive mixture. Rarities, by
definition, don't come by the hundred thousand.
"That's a lot of stamps," I said. "Are they in mixture form, on
paper, in bags, boxes or what?"

"No. They're all organized in stockbooks."

Over the years, I had purchased several large hoards of new issues that turned out to be real treasures, so I asked hopefully, "Are they mint new issues?"

"No, they're used—but they're in good condition," she added. "I discarded the damaged ones as I soaked them off paper." My hopes faded. I visualized Mrs. Nelson working evening after evening, soaking thousands upon thousands of common stamps off paper, then organizing them carefully into stockbooks, which might well turn out to be worth more than the stamps.

"Do you have any idea of their catalogue value?" I asked. It was probably a foolish question, still it never hurt to ask.

"No, I don't have a catalogue value for the entire group yet—but I've started. I've got quite a few better items such as Roman States, Heligoland, German States, and a beautiful set of Samoa Express stamps."

I groaned silently. She had just run down a list of the most commonly encountered reprints, fakes, and forgeries. The genuine articles catalogued big bucks, but the reprints and fakes were basically worthless. "Any other key items?" I asked, still hopeful.

She was silent for a moment—thinking. "Well, nothing as expensive as the ones I mentioned, but there are better stamps here and there. The specifics just don't come to mind at the moment."

By that time I'd pretty much decided that the collection was not worth risking airfare to see. Nothing Mrs. Nelson had said sounded promising.

"Why not have a local dealer look at your stamps?" I suggested.

"I've called all the local dealers, but none of them will come out to see it." Her comment only reinforced my negative impression. Dealers are usually aware of significant holdings in their immediate area—and of turkeys. The accumulation must be worse than I thought if none of the local dealers was willing to drive across town to look at it. I certainly didn't intend to fly hundreds of miles for the privilege.

"I saw your ad and thought maybe you could help me."

"I'd like to, Mrs. Nelson, but the collection just doesn't sound like it would justify the expense of a trip. It would have to be worth at least $5,000 to offset the cost of airfare. From what you've told me, it doesn't sound like it's in that category."

"Oh, I think it is," she countered. "I think you'd be surprised once you got here." The trouble was, I didn't want to be surprised, especially unpleasantly. My instinct told me the collection was a loser and that she no doubt had an exaggerated idea of its value. I didn't want to risk airfare on it.

I made a suggestion. "Let me check with a couple of dealer friends. Maybe one has a trip to Phoenix scheduled. If so, perhaps he could stop by and take a look at your stamps."

I took her telephone number and promised to get back to her in a few days.

I checked with dealer friends who made frequent buying trips, but none planned to be in Phoenix nor were any willing to risk a trip based on my description of the accumulation. I really couldn't blame them. They drew the same conclusion I had.

Mrs. Nelson called me before I had a chance to call her back.

"I'm sorry, but none of the dealers I've spoken to is planning to be in Phoenix," I reported. "Are you sure none of the local dealers will come to your home?" I found it surprising that no one in Phoenix was willing to look at her stamps. After all, it was only a trip across town.

"Yes," she sighed, and then with sarcasm, "They just can't be bothered."

"Tell you what," I said. "I'd be happy to take a look at the collection next time I'm in Phoenix." If I could see her while in town on other business, I'd have no airfare at risk.

She responded with a great, slow sigh of resignation and an unexpected comment, "I really don't want to sell my stamps." She remained silent for a long moment, as if the comment had slipped out unintentionally and she was not sure whether to go on or not. When she finally continued, her words flooded out, like water through a burst dam. "I have some medical expenses coming up in the next couple of weeks, and I need to raise money to meet them. My stamp collection is really the only way I have to do it. I *know* I have good stamps. There's just so many . . . I don't know how to go about making you understand. I can't remember them all and I get the impression you think they're all junk. Well, they're not!" Her voice rose with frustration and anger. "What's the matter with you guys, anyway? You're supposed to be dealers—why won't you come out and make me an offer?"

Then she sounded as if on the verge of tears. "I've been working like crazy to get them organized, putting them in stockbooks so they'd be easy to price. But no one will even come out and see what I've got. I don't know what to do!" Then the line went silent. It was a heavy, liquid silence, the kind that lies quietly at the edge of a vortex, the kind that no one dares break for fear of being drawn into the whirlpool and pulled under. Mrs. Nelson seemed to be at her wit's end, and my heart went out to her. Still, I wasn't sure what to say or do.

At last, I cleared my throat and not really sure where the conversation was going, asked, "How many stockbooks do you have?"

"More than a hundred."

I'll never know why I said what I said next. It just seemed like the right thing. "Okay, I'll come out and take a look." Maybe I'm just a soft touch for a hard-luck story.

"Thank you," she said softly. She sounded genuinely grateful.

"I can get away day after tomorrow if that's convenient. I'll catch an early flight and try to get back the same afternoon." Phoenix is only an hour away from Denver by air, and I didn't want to incur the expense of a motel.

"That would be great! I'll meet you at the airport."

It was mid-August and absolutely the worst time of year to fly to Phoenix, especially on a wild-goose chase. Mrs. Nelson met me at the gate, and when we stepped out of the terminal, the furnace-like blast of air reminded why I don't like Phoenix in the summer.

Mrs. Nelson was a thin woman in her early forties who looked as if she hadn't gotten a good night's sleep in months. She chain smoked and couldn't seem to sit still. I tried to chat with her on the way to her home, but the conversation was rather one-sided. She didn't have much to say.

Her accumulation turned out to be gigantic—stockbook upon stockbook jammed so full of stamps that they wouldn't close properly. Much of the material was common, as I had suspected, but the stockbooks contained great variety and not nearly as much duplication as I had expected. And to my surprise, the stockbooks were marbled throughout with better, medium-priced stamps. The accumulation was much nicer than Mrs. Nelson had made it sound on the phone. Also, to my surprise, she had catalogued much of it, which helped considerably in making an offer. I spent a couple of hours reviewing the stockbooks. When I had finished, my figures totaled $6,500, much more than I thought they would.

"What about these? The $50,000 worth of Roman States and rarities?" she asked, picking up a small red stockbook, opening it to reveal rows of high-catalogue stamps, all of which were fakes or reprints.

"You keep them. They're all fakes or reprints."

"Are you sure they're not worth anything?"

I shook my head no. "That's why you're going to keep them. If I took them, you would always wonder how much they were really worth. So hang on to them. Frame them. Make a display—$50,000 worth of rare stamps."

She smiled at the thought and said, "Okay." Then, setting the red stockbook of pseudo-rarities aside, she said, "I'll take your offer." Suddenly she didn't look as tired and gaunt. She looked relieved. She would have the money she'd need for her medical expenses. I, too, was pleased. The accumulation had proved to be worthwhile, and I was glad that I'd been able to help her. The trip had not been wasted. I still wonder why the local dealers refused to drive across town to see her stamps. Oh well, their loss was my gain.

The point is that Mrs. Nelson's telephone description was so vague that everyone, even the local dealers, assumed the worst. That's why it is essential to describe your stamps adequately on the phone. You risk failing to capture the interest of the best buyer if you're not able to communicate your collection's virtues.

Cases of telephone understatement are not uncommon. I came close to passing up a beautiful collection right in my own backyard because the description sounded so bland. The call came from an elderly gentleman who lived about 60 miles north of Denver. He described his collection succinctly. It contained mint U.S. stamps going back to the 1920s, plus a few earlier items. They were mounted in a Scott National Album. He had started collecting back in the 1930s and had kept the collection up-to-date by buying new issues at the post office over the years. It sounded like yet another routine collection of modern stamps with little value above that of postage. I suggested that he bring it to my office, but he declined. He couldn't make the trip due to his age. I took his number and promised to call back when I had a free morning to drive out to his home.

The trouble is, when you're busy, time flies, and when he called back a couple of weeks later, I realized just how quickly. I apologized for not getting back to him promptly.

"Can you come by this week?" he asked.

I struggled with an answer. The words "Why don't you try another dealer?" were on the tip of my tongue. Business was booming and no matter how hard I worked, the days never seemed to have enough hours. I didn't want to waste half a day driving 60 miles into the country for a marginal collection.

Before I could speak, he said, "Well, you said you'd come and I've been counting on it. We're moving into a retirement home, and I really need to get things wrapped up."

I could tell from the tone of his voice that he felt I'd made a binding commitment, one he expected me to honor in a timely fashion. Put that way, I couldn't say no. I'd said I'd come—so I would. We made an appointment for the following week.

The collection turned out to be a gem. It was loaded with mint stamps and blocks from the 1910s on, all in fantastic condition. He had begun the collection in the 1930s, but worked diligently to acquire earlier stamps as well, at a time when they could be had cheaply. Seldom had I seen a collection mounted with such great care. My mouth watered at page after page of bright, fresh, mint Washington-Franklins, first airmails, Zeppelins, and parcel posts. They looked as if they had been printed yesterday. We made a deal on the spot for $35,000.

I can only surmise that his initial description sounded so lackluster because he had acquired the key stamps at near face value, albeit decades ago. He didn't seem to regard them with the same degree of awe as someone would if they had spent a lot of money for them.

Dealers quickly learn that there are ten duds for every worthwhile collection. So they tend to be skeptical. Dealers also assume that those who have valuable stamps will be quick to point out their prized possessions, while those who do not will be vague and inarticulate in their descriptions.

In summary, before a dealer agrees to travel, he'll want to be sure that your collection meets his minimum—usually $5,000 to $10,000—*and* that you're ready to do business. Take time to organize information about your collection before you invite a dealer to travel. He'll base his decision on what you're able to tell him.

GETTING TO YES

This chapter is devoted to the strategy of getting to yes. The advice is confined to that which applies to stamp transactions. You may find one of the many books on the general subject of negotiating additionally useful, however, negotiating a stamp sale need not be complicated. After all, both you and the stamp dealer want the same thing: to do business. The best advice is to keep things simple. When it comes time to talk business, be straightforward and businesslike. Know what you want and make the dealer aware of your goals. Avoid playing games. They only distract from the real issues, and, all too often, get in the way of making a deal. Examples of some of the more commonly encountered foolishness are given below.

THE TEST

The "test" is a gambit well known to the stamp dealing fraternity. It goes something like this.

"What can you give me for these stamps?" the seller asks, offering a few items, a set of second-rate Zeppelins among them. "If your offer's high enough, I might consider selling you the rest. I want to test your fairness," the cautious seller explains. "Give you an opportunity to prove that you pay the highest prices. Treat me right on these and perhaps we'll do business on the rest."

The seller then hints about the size and quality of his collection, one built over many years, but is a bit vague when it comes to specifics. "You know, I bought much of it years ago and put it away. I haven't looked at it in ages—too busy with business. But I know there's a lot of good material there," he says. *Bought years ago and put away* evokes an image of older, desirable stamps bright and fresh as the day they were printed. Hints of philatelic treasure capture a dealer's attention instantly; they are as irresistible as the fresh scent of fox is to hounds.

"Are Columbians worth much these days?" the seller asks tantalizingly.

"Sure," the dealer answers. "Which ones do you have? Any high values?"

"I don't remember exactly, but I know I've got some of the good ones," he replies, wrinkling his brow slightly as if trying to push the cobwebs of time aside. "I've got some beautiful Trans-Mississippis too," he adds for good measure. The dealer visualizes singles and blocks, all perfectly centered, with bold, crisp colors. Nothing gets a stamp dealer's juices going more than the hint of a quality, old-time collection. But no matter how hard he's pressed, the seller remains vague and indefinite: *Perhaps* we'll do business on the rest; I *might consider* selling the rest. Instead of concentrating on the heavily hinged, off-centered Zeppelins on the table in front of him, the dealer flirts with visions of the mother lode waiting—if he can just pass muster.

Rising to the challenge, the dealer quotes a liberal price for the rag-tag Zeppelins, a price guaranteed to put all others to shame. Judging by the speed with which the seller accepts, he knows well the value of his second-rate Zeppelins. "You have been fair," the seller confides with a smile of approval. "I can see that you pay honest prices." Honest, indeed—the dealer has paid nearly full retail for the Zeppelins; he'll be lucky to make anything at all on them. Still, he deems the expenditure worthwhile if it secures the opportunity to buy the rest of the collection.

"When can I see the balance?" the dealer asks, having demonstrated his good faith.

"Soon," the seller replies, tucking the dealer's check into his pocket. "I'll have to get it organized. I haven't had it out in years. Give me a few weeks. I'll give you a call."

Needless to say, the dealer never hears from him again. Stamp dealers who have been around any length of time are familiar with the "test" and fail to be enticed by it. For my own part, when approached with the test, I simply respond that I'm not interested and let the seller know why. The reason is incentive. The greatest incentive to pay a liberal price is the opportunity to buy the entire collection. That and that alone motivates me to stretch my offer. Buying a few items at high prices in anticipation of doing business on the balance is no incentive at all.

And on those occasions when additional material is forthcoming, I have found it to be nowhere near as nice as the sample. It seems that those inclined to use the test always choose the best items from their collections for the test. Don't be surprised when dealers refuse to be "tested." They are fully aware of the two most likely outcomes: either they'll never hear from the seller again or the balance will be third-rate material. Neither is an incentive.

THE BLUFF

The "bluff" is another popular bit of foolishness. The bluffer names his asking price, usually unrealistically high, then makes the mistake of attributing it to another dealer. Perhaps he is embarrassed to admit that it is his own asking price, or perhaps he believes that attributing it to a dealer gives it more credence. Whatever the reason, the bluff goes something like this.

"I can give you $1,200," the dealer offers, having totaled up the collection.

"I've got another offer of $2,500," the seller snorts in response. The dealer has looked the collection over carefully. He knows the market. He knows how much other dealers pay. He's made a competitive offer. He knows the value of this collection—it's not worth $2,500.

"I'd take the $2,500 and run," the dealer advises. "It's more than I can pay." Unfortunately, the seller doesn't really have a $2,500 offer; $2,500 is far more than the stamps are worth at retail. He's bluffing.

Had the seller been straightforward in the beginning, the dealer might have been willing to spend a little time explaining his offer and the market. Instead, the seller insisted that the phantom price was a legitimate offer, a strategy that put him in an embarrassing position because it was so patently false. The bluffer made the mistake of negotiating as if it were a game, as if the mere bandying about of figures, rather than the real value of the stamps, determined the selling price. Since the seller approached the transaction in an insincere manner, the dealer responds in kind, decides to let him play the game out.

"Well, that offer was made last month, when I was out on the coast," the seller says, no longer as confident as he had been. "I won't be going back there for a while." The more he talks, the deeper he digs his hole.

"You could always ship them," the dealer suggests. Both of them know there is no such bona fide offer.

"I could, but I don't trust the mails," the seller counters lamely. "Besides, I need the money right away. I don't have time to wait for a check." The bluffer plays the part of the exasperated seller well, unaware that the dealer has heard the same story many times before. The seller doesn't know it, but the dealer is enjoying his performance.

"I suppose I could take a loss. Could you go $2,000?" he asks, feigning a pained expression. The loss to which he refers is hypothetical; it is the difference between the $2,500 he wants and the $2,000 he is now willing to take.

"Sorry, can't do it," the dealer replies, shaking his head. "I gave you my best price. If you can get more elsewhere, then by all means, take it." The seller's bluff has been called and he's squirming. He has two choices: he can take the $1,250 and look like a fool for turning down twice as much elsewhere, or he can save face and leave empty-handed.

"Who made the $2,500 offer?" the dealer inquires. "At the prices he's willing to pay, I've got all kinds of stamps I'd like to sell him!"

"Gosh, his name's right on the tip of my tongue," the seller says, hand on his forehead as if trying to remember. "You know . . . the fellow out on the coast. I've got his name written down at home. Damn, the name escapes me," he mutters in mock dismay. There's a pause. Then, "Would you consider $1,750?"

"No, I wish I could, but the stamps aren't worth it to me." Although he might normally negotiate upward from his price, the dealer has decided not to budge because of the seller's tactics—even if it means not buying the collection.

"Well, I was really hoping we could do business," the seller says, arranging his albums as if to leave. "I guess I'll just have to send them out to the coast." He rises slowly and starts for the door. Perhaps he thinks the dealer will call him back at the last moment.

"Good luck," the dealer says.

The seller reaches the door, opens it, and pauses. "Sure you don't want to change you mind?" he asks, looking back at the dealer.

"Positive. Thanks anyway," the dealer responds. The door closes behind the bluffer. Half an hour later he's at another dealer's place of business, and the charade begins anew.

THE WIGII DISCLAIMER

Among the tritest of clichés is the WIGII (What I've Got In It) disclaimer. The WIGII disclaimer is used by sellers to forward the argument for their price, in effect, setting a floor below which they cannot go. More often than not, the figure is invented, nothing more than a negotiating ploy.

Why is WIGII detrimental? Because it has absolutely nothing to do with what a buyer is willing to pay and, in fact, often gets in the way of making a deal. Buyers base their offering prices on the worth of an item to them, not what the seller has paid for it. If the seller overpaid, that's his problem. Quoting a high WIGII price rarely accomplishes what is intended. Instead, the seller burns his bridges. He inhibits the buyer from making any further offers. Any skilled negotiator knows that they key to success lies in keeping negotiations open. WIGII only shuts them off.

Then there's the question of esteem. The logic behind WIGII is that only a fool sells for a loss. Some of the WIGII figures I've heard were so ridiculous that I could only assume that the seller was a complete fool for paying so much, and being a fool, it would therefore be useless to negotiate with him.

On any number of occasions, I've had offers summarily rejected with the indignant remark, "That's less than I've got in it. Do you know what I've got in?" My response is always the same: "I don't want to know! Please don't tell me." Invariably that evokes a look of surprise. How could a dealer not want to be privy to a seller's most sensitive secret? But the truth is, I don't want to know the WIGII figure because it has absolutely no bearing on my offering price, and only creates a barrier to further negotiations.

I know of no professional who actually believes WIGII disclaimers. A seller can quote any figure that suits him. Many years back, at a large stamp show, a dealer—whom I liked, respected, and thought I knew well—had an imperforate error sheet displayed under glass at his bourse table.

"How much?" I asked.

"For you, $2,100," he replied. It sounded a bit steep. Perhaps my expression revealed my surprise, because he added quickly, "I'm asking $2,500 retail."

"I'll pass," I said. "Thanks anyway."

But he was not about to let me get away that easily. "I just bought it—for nearly that much," he persisted. "Look, I've got $2,000 in it," he confided, his tone sincere. "I'm only making a hundred bucks, but a hundred's enough on a quick turn."

I declined again, thanked him, and walked off. Later that day, I mentioned the imperforate sheet to another dealer at the show. To my surprise, he volunteered that he had sold the very same sheet to my erstwhile friend for $1,000 the day before.

The first dealer had lied. I never mentioned that I knew what he had really paid for the sheet, nor have I ever done business with him again. His WIGII disclaimer had no bearing on what I thought the sheet was worth. The price I had in mind—$1,250—was based on what I thought I could reasonably expect to get at retail—$1,500. His WIGII figure preempted any negotiation and, in fact, cost him my future business. To this day, I never believe a WIGII figure.

Stamp dealers buy based on what they can afford to pay for an item, not what someone else has invested in it. WIGIIs are irrelevant. Steer clear of them whether you're a novice or a professional.

I DON'T NEED THE MONEY

Another commonly encountered negotiating disclaimer is "I don't need the money." The remark is, no doubt, prompted by a miscalculation on the seller's part that an offer will be based on his perceived vulnerability rather than on the merits of his stamps.

The vast majority of stamp transactions are not distressed sales. I am not aware of any dealer who operates on the assumption that they are. Again, most dealers recognize that they are in a competitive marketplace and make offers based on the best price they really can afford to pay.

One dealer friend of mine, who can have an acid tongue when he wants to, responds to "I don't need the money" with this reply: "Great! That makes us even, because I don't need the stamps."

THE THREAT

Occasionally, but not frequently, encountered is "the threat," a most ridiculous bit of behavior that defies logic. The seller, angry at the dealer's offer, threatens to use his stamps on mail or even destroy them, as if doing so will somehow punish the dealer. I vividly recall one such episode.

"Are you interested in errors?" the seller asked, handing me a plastic stocksheet containing a misperforated recent commemorative. As I looked at it, he volunteered, "I've got the rest of the sheet and lots more." With that he pulled several stocksheets from his briefcase and spread them out on my desk. They were filled with EFOs (errors, freaks, and oddities): minor perforation shifts, corner folds, shifted colors, and the like.

"Are you interested?" he pressed. I looked them over, rubbing my chin. They were interesting, but I could easily live without them. EFOs, while fascinating, are by no means rare or worth big money. Yet I got the impression from his attitude that he thought they were quite valuable.

"Perhaps," I replied. I wondered where he had gotten them. It is unusual for one person to have found so many EFOs. "You're quite lucky. Most people don't find even one EFO in a lifetime."

"Oh, I work at the post office. I find them every so often and put them aside. How much will you give me for them?"

"They're cute, but not particularly valuable. They're not in the same league as major errors—imperfs, colors omitted, inverts."

He frowned.

"I'm not saying they're valueless, just not worth big bucks," I said. "Finders often have an inflated idea of EFO values, so I prefer not to make offers on them." I handed the stocksheets back to him. "If you have a price in mind, I'll listen."

"No," he replied. "You make me an offer."

"I'll have to pass." The last EFO seller who'd stopped in had wanted $1,000 for a sheet of misperfed stamps, a figure far in excess of its value. Trying to explain that it wasn't worth that much only seemed to make the man suspicious, as if I were trying to trick him. So I passed on it.

"Okay, then I'm going to turn them in for destruction," the postal clerk said vituperatively, as if destroying them would somehow punish me. His logic escaped me. Before he had come in, I had no EFOs. After he left, I would have no EFOs. I would be exactly where I started. The only thing I could possibly lose was a hypothetical profit from not buying his EFOs. On the other hand, he had his stamps. Someone would buy them; it just wouldn't be me. If he destroyed them, he'd have nothing and only harm himself. The logic escaped me.

"That's your decision," I replied. He jammed the stocksheets back into his briefcase and left in a huff.

It is not unusual for sellers to become upset with dealers who decline to buy their collections. Usually such collections are of marginal value and of little interest to the dealer. I have had people threaten to burn their stamps, give them to charity, or use them on mail. One woman even called back to tell me she that she had melted down her accumulation of 24-karat gold-foil stamp replicas after I had declined to buy them.

Threatening to destroy your stamps in an attempt to somehow punish a dealer is a waste of time—the dealer doesn't care.

THE COY SELLER

In almost all cases, sellers have a figure in mind—even if they haven't had an appraisal— but are usually unwilling to reveal it. That is a mistake. If you have an idea of how much you want, don't be coy about it.

The first rule of negotiating a stamp sale is: Always state your asking price. Be prepared to quote it unhesitatingly. Give some thought to it before visiting a dealer. State your asking price before the dealer starts his evaluation. It will give him a target to shoot for as he inspects your stamps. If he comes up short, he'll go through it a second time to see if he can stretch to meet your price.

When the dealer doesn't know your price—the target he must reach for—he'll figure the collection conservatively. *I can state categorically that the figure he arrives at by his own estimate will always be lower than the figure you had in mind, but were reluctant to reveal. Always.* And that principle applies to all transactions—automobiles, antiques, whatever. Call it the Iron Law of Offers: *If you are unwilling to state a price for your goods, you will be offered less than the price you secretly had in mind. Always.*

Sellers are reluctant to quote their asking price due to the misguided notion or hope that a dealer's offer will be more than they had in mind. And there seems to be no undercutting that unrealistic expectation. *In fact, the opposite is true.* You're just asking for a low offer by feigning ignorance. You get respect from a buyer by letting him know your price.

As a youngster, one of the first rules of chess strategy I learned was: *Never surrender the initiative.* The same applies to selling your collection. By quoting a price, you take the initiative. The buyer must try to find a way to meet your price, even if it's more than he might have otherwise paid.

If you have a figure in mind, don't be afraid to quote it. Don't be afraid to quote a price that would make you happy. If it's way out of line, the dealer will quickly set you straight. On the other hand, if he accepts your asking price, you got exactly what you wanted. If he makes an unacceptable counteroffer, you're under no obligation to take it. If you're getting more than one offer, don't be afraid to say so. But be sure to let the dealer know you are ready to do business if his offer is the best.

If you really don't have a figure in mind or don't know what your collection is worth, then say so. Ask for an appraisal and be ready to pay for it. In any case, be straightforward.

Don't reveal the amount of the other offer(s) until after you have received his offer. If it's less than the best offer, give him the opportunity to beat it. Tell him that in fairness to the others, you cannot let the collection go for a token increase. Advise him that you are prepared to do business for ten percent more (or whatever number seems reasonable). He is much more likely to negotiate earnestly if he knows it may lead to a deal right then. As a general rule, dealers don't like to negotiate hypothetically because they have nothing to gain by it. Nothing annoys them more than to agree to a higher price, only to have the seller say he'll think about it. Don't expect a dealer to negotiate in good faith if you're not willing to.

The dealer may not agree to the increase you've asked for. He may counter or he may not budge (it often happens). If he counters, you will have to decide whether his counteroffer is the best you can do. If the dealer really seems to be eager to buy your stamps, but refuses to increase his offer, it's fair to assume that you have pushed him as high as he will go. At that point, you will have to rely upon your own good judgment.

RAISES

Negotiating the best possible price is part of getting to yes, however don't expect large raises. I know of no dealer who offers only a small fraction of what he's really willing to pay. That's not to say that once you have a figure that seems reasonable, you can't try to negotiate an extra five to ten percent. Nominal increases are part of negotiating. Just don't expect an offer to be doubled or substantially raised; it just doesn't work that way. Most dealers offer a price fairly close to what they are actually willing to pay. They may be willing to increase it by ten percent or so, but rarely much more.

As mentioned in previous chapters, it is possible for offers to vary from one dealer to another, especially when specialized or esoteric material is involved. If you've been offered $2,500 for material that you have reason to believe should be worth $4,000, get additional offers. Don't hammer the dealer who offered $2,500 with the expectation that he'll raise his offer to $4,000. It just won't happen.

In summary, be straightforward, direct, and businesslike. Don't hesitate to state your asking price. Remember, dealers tend to base their offers on the market, their own needs, and a property's profit potential, not on whether you need money, what you've got in it, a bluff, or a hypothetical test. These and other irrelevant arguments only create an atmosphere of insincerity and mistrust. They distract from the useful, essential elements of negotiation which are: the market value of the stamps, what you want for them, and whether a dealer's offer is competitive. Sincerity and good faith are essential to mutual respect in any transaction. A sincere approach is usually met with a sincere response. There is nothing a dealer likes less than a seller who insists on playing games. Remember, stamp dealers meet the public every day; they've heard every story in the book. Don't embarrass yourself with a lot of foolishness.

Selling error stamps

Few stamps excite the imagination as much as error stamps—and few are as tricky to buy or sell. Every stamp collector dreams of finding a major error such as the sheet of inverted Jenny airmails purchased by William T. Robey in 1918 from a Washington, D.C. post office. Inverted Jennies now routinely sell for $100,000 plus.

Errors are divided into two broad groups: major errors and EFOs (errors, freaks, and oddities). Major errors include stamps with perforations omitted (imperforates), color(s) omitted, a design element inverted, or a stamp printed in the wrong color. EFOs refer to random production irregularities such as paper foldovers and creases, ink smears, shifted perforations, and the like. Major errors range in price from about $10 to $100,000 plus—depending on rarity. The vast majority of EFOs are worth only a few dollars, although occasionally one may fetch as much as $100 to $200.

Until about 1960, quality control at the Bureau of Engraving and Printing (BEP) was so good that few production errors escaped detection and actually reached the hands of the public. In those days, the BEP relied on visual inspection to weed out incorrectly printed stamps. By the 1960s, however, the demand for stamps had begun to rise dramatically. The increased workload—together with the introduction of increasingly complex and automated printing equipment—curtailed the BEP's ability to visually inspect every sheet of stamps printed. As a result, the number of errors finding their way into public hands burgeoned.

Prior to 1960, only a handful of major errors existed, mostly inverts or imperforates. In the decades following 1960, hundreds of errors surfaced.   At present, the production of coil stamps (stamps sold in rolls) is so automated—from blank paper to finished, packaged roll—that imperforates are assured for every new coil stamp issued for the first class rate.   Imperforate errors coil stamp errors tend to turn up in comparatively large quantities—often hundreds or even thousands of stamps.   Retail prices typically range from $5 to $25 per pair; easily within reach of the average collector.   The proliferation of errors combined with reasonable prices has generated tremendous collector interest, and as a result, a full-fledged error market has developed.

Not every error surfaces in large quantity, and the scarce ones remain expensive.   The value of an error depends largely on the quantity discovered.   That's what makes buying and selling newly discovered errors so tricky.   At the time an error is discovered, it's always unclear how many others might surface.   At that point, the market is completely unpredictable.   Buyer and seller alike operate in the dark.   An error worth $300 one day can be worth $10 the next, and he who holds the stamp is exposed to the risk.

You discover an error.   You're ecstatic!   You pick up the phone and start calling dealers but can't seem to get concrete answers. They sound eager to buy the error, but hedge in response to questions about value.   Instead, they ask how much you want.   You don't know, other than you want as much as possible.   You were counting on them to make an offer.   They hedge.   You come away feeling confused and frustrated.   Maybe they're trying to pull a fast one.   Usually, however, that's not the case.

The complicating factor is that the "value" of an error only becomes established after definite information about quantity becomes known.   Until then a period of uncertainty exists.   Until the market for an error is established, the error's "value" is no more than what buyer and seller agree to.   And that "value" can change overnight.   Dealers with nerves strong enough to specialize in errors know only too well that it's a high-stakes game of Russian roulette.   The following anecdotes give insight into the fast-paced world of buying and selling errors.

Jacques Schiff Jr., the well-known error authority and auction-eer, relates a telling incident.   According to Schiff, a few days after the 15-cent Wreath and Toys Christmas stamp was issued in 1980, he received a call from a collector in Chicago who had discovered a fully imperforate sheet of 50 stamps. Schiff told the excited finder that he had a valuable error, but that it was impossible to estimate its precise value because of its newness. Schiff explained that other error sheets of the same stamp were likely to exist because it had been printed in press sheets of 200, which were then quartered into panes of 50 stamps for sale at post offices. It was possible that at least three other panes—and maybe more—might lie waiting undiscovered in other post offices. Only time would tell how many others would be found. The value of the error depended on the total number to surface. And that could change from day to day.

The caller stressed that his stamps were rarer than the 100 known inverted Jenny airmails and therefore, worth more. His find of 50 stamps would yield 25 pairs (imperforates are collected in pairs). At the time, inverted Jennies were worth $75,000 to $100,000 each (inverts are collected as single stamps).

Schiff pointed out that the inverted Jenny was more than 60 years old, a classic with a proven track record, that no others had ever surfaced, and for those reasons worth $75,000 to $100,000 per stamp. The caller would have none of it. "That may be," he said, "but mine are worth more!" He became irate. He reiterated that his was the only such imperforate sheet in existence—he had checked with several post offices and discovered no others. Schiff knew other sheets could surface anywhere in the country at any time, but chose not argue with him. Normally, Schiff says, he would have offered to sell a pair at unreserved public auction where competitive bidding might have established a realistic value. But he chose not to because of the man's unrealistic attitude toward his perceived multi-million dollar bonanza.

In the intervening years, Schiff says he has purchased and sold 30 or 40 similar imperforate sheets. The first transactions were in the $2,000 per sheet price range; today, $1,000 is a fairer price.

When is the best time to sell? Schiff has good advice for those who discover new errors: "The sooner, the better."

A few years back I received a phone call from a man who had an imperforate roll of one hundred 20-cent flag stamps. "Are you interested?" he asked.

"How much do you want?"

"Four hundred dollars," he replied without hesitation.

"Okay," I agreed. "Ship them."

The roll arrived. It was indeed imperforate. I knew that 20-cent flag imperforates weren't great rarities, but I thought they would make eye-catching stamp-show specials at $12.50 per pair. At the time, these errors catalogued $20 per pair, so the asking price of $8 per pair seemed reasonable.

No sooner had I mailed his check than I received the new *Scott Specialized Catalogue*. You can imagine my distress when I found the catalogue price had been reduced to $8 per pair. I had just paid full retail for the stamps! Many months and many stamp shows later, I was finally rid of the last of them. I sold pairs for less than my cost, recouped a little from the plate number strips, and perhaps broke even on the entire deal. I vowed to be more cautious about buying errors in the future.

Not long after that episode, I received a call from a man offering imperforate coil pairs of the C stamp of 1981. At the time, I had heard of no others turning up imperforate, so I assumed his was the initial discovery. He claimed that the find consisted of just a few pairs and wanted to know how much they were worth. I couldn't tell him and explained why. For all I knew, others might lie awaiting discovery, or others might have been discovered but not yet reported. Until more was known, it would be difficult to value them. I asked him to ship them to me for inspection. I wanted to verify that they were indeed imperforate and contained no blind perfs (partially impressed perforations). He agreed to send them.

The shipment consisted of a small number of strips including one line pair. The stamps, indeed, were imperforate, but the gum along the top edges had been slightly disturbed by moisture. I worried that he might have sent only the first few stamps on a roll of 500. If the balance of the roll was imperforate and not damaged by moisture, I'd end up with the only faulty copies of an error much more common than first thought—and worth much less. The gum disturbance was not severe, but enough to kill sales of the impaired copies if sound ones turned up. Although he assured me that he had sent the entire holding, I wasn't convinced. Sellers have been known to parcel out their error finds to more than one dealer, each of whom thinks he alone is getting the entire find, until the ruse is discovered.

The C stamp had been produced in massive quantities for the first-class letter rate change from 18 cents to 20 cents. Odds favored more imperforate copies surfacing. That, too, gave me pause. Imperforates of both the A and B transitional coil stamps had surfaced in quantities of 200 to 400 pairs. As a result, they were relatively inexpensive. My experience with the plummeting price of 20-cent imperforate flag coil made me wary.

I called back and asked how much he wanted. He didn't know. He wanted me to tell him how much they were worth. The only problem was that I didn't know their value. I tried to explain the uncertain nature of the error market, but without much luck. He seemed to take my vagueness about value for shrewdness. He must have assumed that I knew the value of the error, but hoping to buy them cheaply, wouldn't reveal it to him. For my part, our telephone conversations left me with the impression that he wasn't being completely forthcoming, perhaps even evasive. Or he may have just been cautious and I misinterpreted it. I decided not to make an offer and asked for a few days to think it over.

The imperforate C stamps languished in my desk drawer for nearly two weeks. I hoped that news of other finds would surface and make my decision easier, but none did.

When at last I called him, the conversation went nowhere. He remained suspicious; I remained wary. No matter how hard I pressed him to name a price, he remained vague. The best I could get from him was that he might consider—not accept, but only consider—high hundreds or low thousands per pair. The possibility that additional rolls of the C imperforate might turn up haunted me. For an imperforate coil pair to be worth high hundreds of dollars or low thousands, it would have to be genuinely rare—less than 50 pairs known. The moment several hundred pairs surface, its value drops like a rock, usually to less than $100.

I suggested auctioning a pair to establish a market price, then placing the balance by private treaty, but that didn't appeal to him either. He was worried that the trial pair might not bring a price as high as he thought it should.

At first I thought the mysterious caller was playing his cards close to the vest; later I decided that he was simply indecisive. He really didn't know how much he wanted for his errors, other than it be a concrete figure, the maximum possible retail price per pair. He didn't seem to put much stock in my explanation of how the market operates, nor was he willing to take any risk—even to test the waters at auction. For my part, I wondered how many error pairs he really had. I concluded that the profits, if any, were not worth the risk and headaches of dealing with him. Besides, the odds favored more imperforate C coils surfacing. So I sent his stamps back to him.

The C coil imperforate turned out to be one of the scarcest letter-denominated coils; only those few pairs ever turned up. I had held them all in my hand, but I'm really not sorry I let them go. I have a completely irrational but nagging suspicion that had I bought them at $500 per pair or more, others would have surfaced, and today the error would be worth something like $10 per pair.

In previous chapters, I stressed the value of shopping around for the best offer, however with errors that is not always the best strategy.   Value depends on scarcity.   And perceptions are important.

The error market is extremely sensitive to supply. A doubling of supply from 100 copies to 200 can knock down the price of an error by 75 percent or more. It's possible for a new error to turn up in several parts of the country at about the same time. That possibility makes error dealers cautious about paying too much for newly discovered errors.

Of necessity, error dealers communicate. New discoveries do not remain secret for long. However, while they guard their sources jealously, they do share information about quantities of new errors in order to protect themselves from overpaying.

In the mid-1970s, I got a call from a local fellow with a newly discovered commemorative imperforate error. I won't use his name or reveal the stamp because he wishes to remain anonymous. The point of the story can, nevertheless, be related.

Unlike definitives, commemoratives are produced in relatively small numbers. I knew that if no further sheets surfaced, the commemorative error would be a very expensive item. I explained the error market to him, its fragile nature, and that the sheet should best be managed by distributing individual pairs discretely. I suggested an arrangement in which I would use my best efforts to sell the stamps and share in the profits. He agreed.

What he had failed to tell me before we agreed to do business was that he had telephoned dealers all over the United States inviting offers for his error sheet. Dealers had talked to dealers, who had talked to other dealers, and so on. This resulted in a rumor that several error sheets of 50 existed. Even though no additional sheets had actually surfaced, the weight of the rumors depressed the market. No one wanted to take the chance that the rumors weren't true. Savvy buyers—collector and dealer alike—know that in most cases an error can be obtained later for less than at the time of its discovery. Eventually I sold all the stamps in the error sheet. The result satisfied the finder, but I think we could have gotten a lot more had he not beaten the bushes before coming to me. To this day, years later, at least one error dealer friend of mine still insists that other sheets of that error exist, and that they are being held off the market until the price rises. He's among those who originally received a phone call from the finder.

Bob Dumaine, the well-known Houston, Texas, stamp dealer, relates another interesting story in the same vein. According to Dumaine, he received a call offering a completely imperforate sheet of fifty 1985 poinsettia Christmas stamps. Dumaine knows his way around the error business and understands well the relationship between quantity and value, so he made a point to ask, "Is it the only sheet you have?" The caller said it was. The caller wanted $2,000, a price that did not seem unreasonable for a unique sheet. Dumaine bought it relying on the statement that it was the only sheet.

Dumaine then shared the news of his purchase with fellow error dealer Jack Nalbandian. You can imagine Dumaine's amazement when Nalbandian told him that he, too, had just closed a deal for the only known sheet of the same error. They compared names. Both had been contacted by the same man.

Dumaine telephoned several other error dealers around the country, and in no time at all found out that Jacques Schiff Jr. and Marvin Frey, among others, had also made arrangements to auction or purchase identical sheets, all from the same party. Something, definitely, was rotten in Denmark.

Dumaine called the duplicitous seller and confronted him with the facts. "How could you claim it was the only sheet?" Dumaine demanded. "You actually had several sheets when you called me!"

"It was the only sheet that I had in my hand at that moment," came the lame reply, according to Dumaine, who chuckles in retrospect when relating the story.

The seller was, undoubtedly, lucky that the incident occurred in the twentieth century. Had it happened on the frontier, Dumaine, known for having the "fastest check in the West," certainly would have invited the fellow to meet him on Main Street at high noon. There Dumaine would have demonstrated that a check was not the only thing he was fast with.

I can visualize Dumaine—those who know Bob can best appreciate this description—walking down a dusty Main Street toward the hapless error finder. It's high noon. The Texas sun blazes overhead. Not a cloud mars the sky. Bob's wearing a white Stetson. Spurs jingle on the heels of his alligator-hide cowboy boots. His right hand brushes aside the tan suede of his Yves St. Laurent sport coat revealing the polished ivory butt of a Colt .45. Its whiteness contrasts against the lavender of his Givenchy shirt. Carrera sunglasses hide the fire in his eyes. Dumaine stops twenty paces away from the trembling error finder, waiting for him to make his move. Finally, his patience exhausted, Dumaine says, "Okay, Podna, you done bought the farm, chicken yard and all—draw!"

However, as colorful as he is, it must be said that Bob Dumaine is a reasonable man. So instead, back in the twentieth century, they came to an accommodation; the seller agreed to a substantial reduction in price for all buyers.

Another Dumaine anecdote illustrates well the fragile relationship between quantity and price. The saga of the rise and fall of the AMERIPEX error-stamp booklet certainly ranks as a classic. The action took place in the spring of 1986 at INTERPEX, the New York ASDA show. According to Dumaine, just prior to INTERPEX he bought a single booklet of AMERIPEX stamps with black omitted from another dealer who had two of them. He paid $500. Dumaine took the error booklet to New York knowing that INTERPEX would be an ideal place to sell it. On Thursday, the opening day of the show, Dumaine learned from his office in Texas that someone had called from Pennsylvania offering ten additional AMERIPEX error booklets for sale. Dumaine instructed his office to offer $250 each for them; the offer was accepted.

In the meantime, Dumaine sold his inventory of 11 booklets for $475 each to a dealer whom we'll call E.B. The ten booklets from

Pennsylvania were to be shipped to E.B. as soon as Dumaine's office received them.

No sooner had Dumaine sold the 11 booklets than he got word from his office that a third caller, again from Pennsylvania, had 100 AMERIPEX error booklets for sale. The caller had heard that Dumaine was paying $250 each for them. It was rapidly becoming obvious that the AMERIPEX error booklet was much more common than first known and, therefore, worth much less than $250. Dumaine instructed his office to offer $75 per booklet; the offer was accepted. Back on the floor at INTERPEX, he moved quickly, selling his latest acquisition of 100 booklets to E.B. for $200 each, again to be delivered in due course. It turned out to be a wise move.

Bright and early Friday morning, an individual showed up at INTERPEX with 300 AMERIPEX error booklets for sale. News of the appearance and sale of the latest batch further depressed the market. When the dust had settled, AMERIPEX error booklets were trading in the $75 range at wholesale.

While all of this was going on, still another seller called Dumaine's office in Texas—this time with 500 booklets for sale. The bloom was off the rose. Before making a commitment to buy the latest 500 booklets, Dumaine secured a firm offer of $35 per booklet from E.B. With that commitment in hand, Dumaine offered the phone seller $20 per booklet, which he immediately accepted. It was rumored that E.B. resold that batch of 500 for $50 dollars per booklet. The finder made $18 per booklet, Dumaine made $15 per booklet, and E.B. made $15 per booklet. Rumor had it that E.B. was acquiring the error booklets for a dealer client who had invested heavily in them early on intending to make a market in them, and now found himself having to protect his investment.

By Friday afternoon, the wholesale price of AMERIPEX error booklets had dropped to $15 at INTERPEX. Later the following week, after he had returned to Houston, Dumaine was offered a large lot of additional thousands of AMERIPEX booklets. In the space of a few short days the AMERIPEX error booklet had become one of the most common error items in philatelic history. At this writing, the retail price of the AMERIPEX error booklet has rebounded to and stabilized in the $40 to $50 range.

The moral to the story is twofold: the error market is very fragile, and the best time to sell is early on.

In most cases, the best price is realized at the time of initial discovery; there are few exceptions. Time is of the essence. A newly discovered error is like a hot potato—hold it too long and you risk getting burned. It is axiomatic that the initial finder profits most from an error. The finder pays only face value. Whatever he gets above and beyond that is profit. The dealer/buyer owns the error at an elevated cost basis. He is exposed to the risk of real loss should additional finds surface—a very real risk. He's exposed to that risk all during the time it takes to retail the errors. And even if no others surface, time works against him because prices for newly discovered errors tend to drop in the short term, before beginning to appreciate over the long haul—ten years or more.

If you find an error, move quickly and quietly. Don't make too much noise. You'll only make potential buyers nervous and that drives the price down.

Probably the best approach for disposing of a newly discovered error is to work with a specialist dealer in the error field whom you feel you can trust. In effect, make him your partner. That way the risk is shared. You have the benefit of a professional's expertise, and it is in his best interest to manage the disposition of the error to its maximum yield. Check the philatelic weeklies or the ASDA for those who specialize in errors and actively buy them.

In summary, dealers don't like to gamble on newly discovered errors until it becomes reasonably clear how many exist. There's always the possibility that others will surface. This is especially true for definitive stamps, which are typically in production for several years. The moment more surface, an error's value falls. Because the market is so quantity sensitive, holding a newly discovered error is a risky proposition. Holding an error for the long term makes sense only if you control all known copies, and are willing to gamble that no others will surface. Holding errors for the long term with the expectation of a greater profit later is a long shot. Realizing a higher profit from holding long-term is the rare exception rather than the rule.

It is appropriate to close this chapter with a quote from Bob Dumaine, "Greed—in the field of errors—is the one thing that will end up costing you, rather than making you money."

TO KEEP OR NOT TO KEEP: STAMPS AS INVESTMENTS

This chapter is not about how to invest in stamps. That subject could easily fill a book by itself. However, stamp sellers frequently ask about stamps as investments so the subject is covered here as it applies to the most commonly asked questions: "Should I hold my stamps?" "Will they increase in value?" and "When will the stamp market boom again?"

Stamps are generally considered good investments. However, as is the case with any commodity, some are and others are not. Many kinds of stamps—approvals, new issues, kiloware, packets, mixtures, newly issued commemoratives purchased at the post office, modern mass-produced first day covers, and the like—are not good investments. But they were never intended to be.

Remember, stamp collecting is a hobby, something to be pursued for fun, for the hours of enjoyment and satisfaction it offers. The casual golfer, the gardener, and the model builder expect no profit. Yet when the word "stamps" is mentioned, profit instantly comes to mind. Somewhere along the line, the concept of value eclipsed the concept of hobby when it comes to stamp collecting.

Having said that, one of the advantages of stamp collecting is that when you have finished enjoying the hobby, stamps have residual value. But that value should be regarded as a bonus, not the *raison d'etre* for collecting stamps. And that residual value may be more than the amount originally spent on the stamps, or it may be less. Ironically, the most valuable collections tend to be those formed over a period of years by knowledgeable collectors with little thought to profit. First-rate collections of this kind yield good prices in relation to their original cost; stockpiles of common stamps do not.

Sellers, especially those disappointed by what they feel is a low offer, often wonder whether to hold onto their stamps (hoping that they will appreciate significantly) or sell them. The answer depends on the kind of stamps and the potential return from the proceeds of selling if invested elsewhere.

As mentioned, most stamps are not investment grade. These include low-priced approvals, accumulations of kiloware, packet-material, mixtures, modern mass-produced first day covers, and post-1945 accumulations of mint postage. This last category—post-1945 accumulations of mint postage—causes more misunderstanding than all the others combined.

I can't begin to count the number of times I've checked a run of post-1945 mint sheets or plate blocks and given the seller the bad news: they're postage; good for mailing letters; worth 80 percent of face value on the market.

This news is invariably greeted with the shocked reaction: "Less than face value?!"

"Yes, I'm afraid so."

"But how can that be? Stamps are supposed to be good investments."

"Some are, but post-1945 U.S. mint stamps are among those that are not. Most were issued in quantities of 100 million or more. They continue to be abundant."

"I don't think I want to sell at a loss," the seller frets. "Maybe I'll just keep them. Someday they might be worth more." A pause. "What do you think?"

Unfortunately, time alone will not cause common mint postage to rise in value. Increased demand brought to bear on a limited supply creates rising prices. Demand is the key factor. Rarity is secondary, and age by itself, has little to do with value. In order for post-1945 mint sheets to increase in value, there must be a corresponding expansion of collectors (demand) to absorb the vast squirreled-away hoards (supply).

After World War II, collectors began putting aside extra copies of every new commemorative—ten copies, twenty copies, even sheets or multiple sheets. Each extra sheet (assuming 50 stamps per sheet) created a floating supply of 50 stamps, enough to satisfy the needs of 50 new collectors of single stamps. Unfortunately, the hobby did not—and is not—expanding at a rate anywhere near that necessary to absorb the vast floating supply of these extra millions of stamps. And who knows when, if ever, it will. I'm sure I won't see it in my lifetime. In the meantime, the value of these stamps is merely postage.

The potential seller wants to know: "Should I hold onto mint sheets for future appreciation?" The following anecdote illustrates the futility of holding modern postage hoards.

In 1980, a woman offered me an accumulation of mint sheets with a face value of $10,000. She had received it as part of a legal settlement and had no interest in stamps. She wanted to cash out. I offered $8,000 for the lot. She refused indignantly. "Do you take me for a fool?" she asked.

I explained the market for discount postage and the rationale for holding the stamps versus converting them to cash. Money-market and certificate-of-deposit (CD) yields were as high as 14 percent in those days. I even had my own funds in money market accounts at the time. I pointed out that $8,000 invested in a CD at the then current rate would more than recoup the face value of $10,000 in two years and yield a profit after that.

At this writing [in 1989] a conservative estimate of the value of $8,000 invested in CDs, given the interest rates during the intervening years, would be $16,650—more than double the original $8,000.

But the owner chose not to sell, and the stamps continue to be discount postage still worth only $8,000. I've run into this lady several times over the years, and each time she asks the same question, "Are the stamps worth face value yet?" The answer, too, is always the same: "No." She cannot seem to get beyond the fact that, initially, a slight loss will have to be incurred in order to liquefy the holding. The alternative, holding the stamps for the long run, will be far more costly. In another 10 years, the stamps will still be worth only $8,000, while the value of $8,000—had it been invested in Cds in 1980—is conservatively projected to be $25,000 or more, depending on interest rates.

Owners of modern postage accumulations face a choice between a certain rate of return and the chance (which is extremely remote) that modern mint postage will, over time, appreciate to the same extent. Holding out, waiting for time to work its magic on modern mint sheets, is just not realistic.

A word to the wise: the problem of having to sell at a discount from face value can be avoided by not buying excessive quantities of new issues in the first place. That sounds like philatelic heresy, but few mint sheet buyers stop to consider the long-term results of needless overstocking. It's difficult to dissuade collectors from the old maxim: "You can't go wrong at face." The logic of buying new mint sheets at face is that it is like getting IBM stock at original issue price. In reality, it's the same as acquiring shares of *every* new penny stock issued. For every future blue-chip, there are hundreds of losers.

Don't get me wrong; I'm not knocking stamps. I am knocking uninformed, mindless buying. A more reasoned approach is to buy a single stamp of each new issue if you collect singles, one plate block if you collect plate blocks, and so forth. That way you will spend only a few dollars a year, and the money that you would have tied up in face value duplicates can be more profitably spent acquiring earlier, better stamps. Earlier, better stamps—by virtue of their genuine scarcity—offer the best potential for appreciation.

In summary, base your decision on whether to hold or to sell on the anticipated future value of the stamps versus the future value of their proceeds invested elsewhere.

Another frequently asked question is "When will the stamp market boom again?"

During the late 1970s, when tangible investments were the rage, stamp prices shot through the roof. And best of all, stamps appeared to be depression proof (unlike other assets, they had not decreased in value during the Great Depression). Great upside potential; no downside risk. Stamps seemed to be the perfect investment. If only it were true! What investors failed to realize was that the stamp market didn't crash during the Great Depression because it had not boomed prior to it. The situation was different in the late 1970s when stamp prices seemed to rise almost daily, and it appeared that the boom would go on forever.

Stamps boomed, not because they possessed some innate, sterling quality, but because all tangibles boomed. Stamps rode the coattails of a general, inflation-inspired, bull market in tangibles. Speculative demand for stamps surged, money poured into the market, and prices rose accordingly resulting in a broad speculative bubble—the likes of which the hobby had never seen before. The accompanying chart (Figure 3) illustrates what happened. The solid trend line—based on a cross section of stamps—represents the equilibrium point between supply and demand. Its slope, virtually horizontal (until the speculative bubble), reveals the stamp market as historically flat and non-volatile, increasing only slightly over time. From this, one might deduce that the stamp market is not one inclined to rapid price rises.

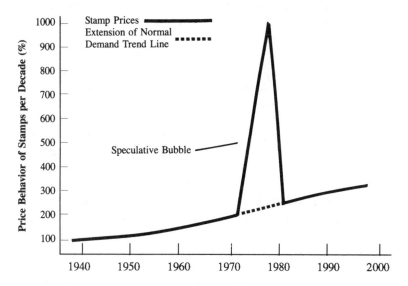

Figure 3. Stamp prices over the decades.

Then suddenly in the 1970s, the trend line climbed sharply from its level path to an Everest-like peak. But unlike Mt. Everest, the stamp market was not rock-solid; it was more like the insubstantial surface of a bubble—a speculative bubble.

The surge in stamp prices was not due to legions of new collectors entering the hobby. It was due to sudden constriction in supply. Everyone wanted to buy and hold stamps; no wanted to sell. Call it greed, call it hedging against inflation, or whatever; the reasons are not important, only the effect—a classic speculative bubble. Wildfire speculation pushed prices to artificially high levels, levels not supported or supportable by basic collector demand. Overall, price gains for the decade were tenfold. It was truly a speculative mania.

Had it not been for speculative mania, the basic trend line would have undoubtedly continued on, smooth and level, as it had over the decades. The dotted line in Figure 3 represents that hypothetical trend line, the likely level of prices had there been no speculative bubble.

In 1980, the speculative bubble burst as all speculative bubbles do. Stamp prices tumbled. Those who believed stamps to be immune from the laws of the free market suffered a rude awakening. They might have known better had they read Charles P. Kindleberger's classic work on the subject, *Manias, Panics, and Crashes*, which traces dozens of speculative manias from 1720 onward including cotton, wheat, public lands, gold, railroads, building sites, coffee, canals, turnpikes, sugar, and tulip bulbs. And in the late 1970s, it was stamps.

As the chart illustrates, once the element of speculation was removed from the equation, the trend line returned to a level approximating that which it would have occupied had there been no speculative mania. Understanding both the equilibrium between supply and demand and the non-volatile nature of the hobby is the key to understanding how the stamp market will behave in the future. Without an influx of new collectors or a renewed interest in stamps as investments, the stamp market will remain steady and the trend line flat.

One more related point. Postal administrations of the world flood the market with torrents of new issues. The multitude of new issues soaks up a lot of the money that would otherwise be available to purchase older stamps. It's entirely possible that siphoning off so much cash has a depressing effect on the demand for and the prices of older stamps.

Will the stamp market boom again? Perhaps, but who knows when? Bear in mind that the bubble of the late 1970s was an anomaly, something that does not recur on a regular basis. So long as the economy remains stable the stamp market likely will continue its traditional sideways movement.

Investment-quality stamps (not modern mint sheets and low-grade junk) held over time will probably match the rates of return on low-yield financial instruments such as savings accounts.

Without runaway inflation, it is unrealistic to expect stamps to rise in value meteorically, as they did in the late 1970s.

As a general rule, consider holding stamps as investments only if you enjoy them. If you don't really care about stamps, convert them to cash and put your money into something you understand. You'll probably have better luck.

If you collect, avoid spending excessive sums on new issues. It's better to go after the earlier, more desirable material. I'm sure that I speak for most stamp dealers when I say that I can't get excited over the hoards of mint sheets that walk through the front door week in and week out. The material is so common and the profit margin so slim, that I really don't care if I buy it or not.

On the other hand, carefully formed, serious collections of any nation or specialty containing balanced runs of premium stamps impress me. I'm eager to buy them for reasons opposite those mentioned above. Organized collections containing keys don't come along every day, and profit margins are better. They're the kinds of properties that dealers stretch to buy. So if you're still collecting, put your money into good individual stamps, not hoards of face value duplicates. You'll not only get more for your efforts, but find it easier to sell your collection when the time comes.

STAMP INVESTMENT IN GENERAL

While we're on the subject of investment, here's some general advice. Stamps are widely regarded as a foolproof investment that requires no knowledge, no homework, and no skill. They're viewed as an investment that can be purchased mindlessly, held for a period of time, and then cashed in for big profits. It's not that easy. Success in stamp investment, as in any field, requires knowledge, constant homework, and experience. Successful investors know what elements cause surges and slumps, they understand timing, and they are aware of the idiosyncrasies of their chosen field. For those reasons, they are successful—not because the object of their investment possesses a special, magical attribute for profit.

If you intend to invest in stamps, go into the field with your eyes open; know what is required of you. Take off your jacket, roll up your sleeves, step into the ring, and understand that it's a bare-knuckle fight. You're going to take some blows. You're going to get bruised. You may get bloodied. And you may even get knocked out. If you're not prepared to take the punches, don't get into the ring.

To be effective you will need to do a lot of studying. You'll need to learn the economics of the stamp market, how dealers value stamps, how markups vary, where to buy, when to buy, how long to hold, when to sell, how to sell, how to recognize speculative situations, and a lot more. You'll not succeed by plunking down a few dollars each week on mint sheets, then forgetting about them with the idea that someday you'll send the kids to college on them.

If you're not willing to exert the effort it takes to become skilled and knowledgeable, you don't stand a chance. You cannot rely on vague generalities such as Chinese stamps will rise in value because there are a billion Chinese who, once they become affluent, will pay dearly for stamps of their homeland. Or that oil-rich inhabitants of Arabian peninsula will take up stamp collecting, rush to buy stamps of their homeland, sending prices through the roof. Perhaps Chinese peasants won't take up collecting en masse, and perhaps of the *nouveau riche* of the Gulf States would rather collect Arabian horses.

To be successful at stamp investing, you will have to rely on your own expertise; you'll have to call your own shots. An old maxim counsels: "A lawyer who represents himself has a fool for a client." The axiom for investors is: "An investor who relies on anyone but himself is a fool." If you have no expertise and are not inclined to get any, don't expect profits. It's that simple.

"YOU CAN'T GO WRONG AT FACE" & OTHER MYTHS

One of the enduring myths of philately is: "You can't go wrong at face." Stocking up on newly issued U.S. stamps is popular with collectors, and the belief that they are good investments, widespread. After all, they can be purchased at the post office for face value—at cost, so to speak—with no apparent downside risk. What could be a better deal?

The notion of newly issued mint stamps as solid investments, no doubt, had its origins in the 1930s. In his book *Nassau Street,* Herman Herst Jr. paints a vivid picture of the rampant speculation in new U.S. mint stamps that occurred during the 1930s and 1940s. During that period, many new issues, driven by speculation, rose rapidly in value—doubling, tripling or increasing even more overnight—only to plunge dramatically after the initial frenzy subsided, never to recover despite the passing of decades.

That speculative behavior was stimulated by a huge expansion in stamp collecting during the 1930s. Stamps were issued less frequently in those days, only a few per year. Each new stamp was an event enthusiastically anticipated by collectors, who eagerly stocked up on duplicates. World War II temporarily curtailed commemorative stamp production, but after the war the floodgates opened. Collectors awash in postwar prosperity purchased them with the single-minded passion of one who believes he's found the secret to instant wealth. They purchased multiples—two, five, even ten sheets or plate blocks at a time. They tucked them away for the day when they would be worth big money. All these years later, that day has still not yet arrived.

I clearly remember the day I realized that three-cent plate blocks would never be scarce—at least not during my lifetime. I had been invited to make an offer on the estate of a small-town postmaster. He had salted away tens of thousands of plate blocks, all sorted into bundles of 100 alike, and then neatly banded into bricks of 1,000—*bricks of 1,000 alike!* How many other hoards like that one exist? I have no idea. However, the message is clear. There are more than enough post-1945 plate blocks to go around.

The urge to buy at face value and hoard still prevails even today. Can you go wrong at face? Indeed you can, as many have learned the hard way. A while back, I got a call from a fellow with an accumulation of mint sheets.

"I've got some mint sheets for sale. Are you interested?"

"Perhaps," I replied. "How far back do they go?"

"About ten years. They're mostly commemoratives."

"How much in face value?"

"About two hundred thirty-four."

"Your best bet is to use them on mail," I said. "I'm paying 80 percent of face value at the moment. You could shop them around. You might find a slightly better price, but considering the small amount, you might as well use them on mail."

"Eighty percent of face?!" he said, his voice full of annoyance. "I thought stamps were supposed to increase in value?"

"The earlier, scarcer ones do," I replied. "And perhaps yours will be worth a premium someday, but that's not likely anytime soon." Then, as I had done so many times before, I found myself explaining the market for mint sheets. "Most stamps issued since World War II are still common even today and typically trade at a discount. The problem is oversupply. Collectors put away sheets and sheets of new issues, far more than the secondary market requires. For some reason, the notion persists that newly issued mint sheets are a good investment.

"We don't make much on discount postage," I continued. "It's not sold to collectors at large markups. Most of it ends up going to commercial mailers. We pay 80 to 85 percent and re-sell to mailers at 90 to 92 percent. Without the 7 to 10 percent incentive each, neither mailers nor dealers would bother with it. And consider this. If the Postal Service suddenly demonetized old stamps, there wouldn't be much demand for them at all.

"And lately," I further explained, "a lot of business mailers, who at one time were eager to use discount postage, have lost interest, despite the savings, because of the inconvenience. Who wants to struggle with all the odd denominations—three-, four-, six-, eight-, ten-, thirteen-, eighteen-, twenty-two-cent stamps—to make useful combinations? It's too much trouble. My advice is to just use your stamps on mail."

"But there's too many," the caller said, which surprised me, because I had the impression that he owned a business.

"You have a business, don't you?"

"Yes."

"Well then, just use them on your mail. I go through a couple of hundred dollars worth of postage a month. It shouldn't take long to use $234 worth."

"Not $234 worth," he said in exasperation. *"I have $234,000 worth."*

It was my turn to be stunned.

"How did you end up with so many?" I asked, struggling to grasp the magnitude of his holding.

"I bought a pad of every new issue," he replied. (A pad is a post-office package of 100 sheets. For example, the face value of a pad of 15-cent commemoratives, assuming 50 stamps per sheet, is $750. Buying a pad at a time adds up quickly.)

"A pad of every new issue?" I repeated incredulously. "Why?"

"Thought it would be a good investment. Everyone told me stamps were a good investment. Now you're telling me that I can get only eighty percent of face value," he said, his voice rising with anger. I couldn't blame him. Not only would he not make a profit, he stood to lose a sizable amount on the deal. On the other hand, he should have taken time to learn more about the stamp market before plunging in headfirst—especially with megabucks.

"The size of your holding changes things," I said. "A lot that large takes time for the market to absorb. My guess is that you're going to be lucky to get seventy percent, and you may have to take terms—payment in installments, perhaps no money for the first ninety days or so."

"Seventy percent!" he shouted. "I'll keep the damn sheets before I turn them loose for that kind of money." The phone burned my ear, still I couldn't blame him for being angry. He faced a potential loss of $75,000—more money than most collectors spend on stamps in a lifetime. How misleading is the old adage "You can't go wrong at face."

I don't know what he finally did with his accumulation of mint sheets. I recall seeing a booth covered with pads and pads of commemoratives—all priced at face value—stacked like so much bargain-basement merchandise at one of the New York ASDA shows. Perhaps he had found a buyer, or perhaps it was yet another mint sheet hoard.

Mint sheets are not the only items that appear to be good investments that, instead, return less than their original cost. A few years back, I received shipment of nearly a dozen large, weighty cartons loaded with covers (cover is a philatelic term for an envelope). The owner had gone completely hog wild over mass-marketed mail-order first day covers. It looked as if he had responded to every direct-mail offer he'd ever received. The cartons held dozens and dozens of albums containing hundreds upon hundreds of covers. Some bore beautiful full color cachets, some contained gold-foil stamp replicas, and many had been "personalized" with the owner's name typed on, a practice that actually decreases value because most first day cover collectors prefer unaddressed covers. In addition to first day covers, the accumulation contained special Bicentennial sets, U.S. Presidents commemorative sets, state capitals sets, and on and on—all lavishly presented, each cover individually mounted on an attractive page containing flowery paragraphs about the event commemorated. Most sets of these "designer covers" contained endorsements from official organizations and societies and of course, the ubiquitous certificates of authenticity—although I can think of no reason why such prosaic material requires certification.

Unfortunately, designer covers are not prized by the traditional collector. In fact, veteran collectors generally hold them in low esteem and argue that they exploit the public. As a result, there is little secondary market for them, regardless of how attractive they are.

Designer covers are mass-marketed (typically by direct mail or through advertisements in Sunday newspaper supplements) to the philatelically unsophisticated, who—more often than not—regard them as good investments even though they are not necessarily represented as such. Priced at $2 to $5 each, they are inexpensive in relation to the cost of living; however, they are quite expensive considering that similar covers retail for 50-cents to $1 each in the secondary market. Grandparents put them away for grandchildren. Parents buy them thinking that someday the proceeds will send the kids to college. Sadly, the only school most designer covers ever purchase admission to is the school of hard knocks.

In fairness, the free market allows any entrepreneur to offer products to the public. Besides, there are those who argue that anything that serves to broaden the population of potential stamp collectors is good for the hobby. So it's up to the buyer to investigate products he contemplates purchasing for investment. The wisdom of the marketplace first put forward in ancient Rome still applies today: *Caveat emptor!*

Getting back to the story, I calculated their value of the covers and called the owner. "The collection is worth about a thousand dollars—" I began.

"A thousand dollars!?" he interjected angrily. "I paid over ten thousand dollars for those covers. I have the receipts. You damn stamp dealers are all the same—nothing but a bunch of crooks!"

There was no use continuing the conversation. I was not about to be insulted. "I'll send the covers back today," I said, anxious to conclude the unpleasantness.

"Where do you come off offering less than a dime on the dollar?" he persisted.

I really didn't want to discuss the matter, nevertheless I could not resist asking, "Have you offered them back to the firms you bought them from?"

"Yes. They won't buy them back."

"Doesn't that tell you something?"   A moment of silence followed.   "If they're such desirable property, why won't the issuers buy them back?"

Another long moment of silence, then he said, "They only issue them, I guess."

"Right!" I said. "They sell them by the thousands to buyers like you, but they won't buy them back. The fact is that everyone interested in owning them buys them new, from the source. The colorful brochures tell you how wonderful these are—endorsed, certified, heirloom quality, and on and on. What they don't tell you is that there is virtually no secondary market for them. Yet you expect me and other dealers like me to buy your covers at fancy prices despite the fact we have no customers for them. Well, that's not the way it works." The more I spoke, the angrier I became. Too many times had I been the unfair object of wrath from designer cover owners. My cumulative irritation boiled over. I unloaded on the caller.

"Then when I tell you what your covers are really worth, you get mad at me. Well, I'm not the one who took your money, and I really don't want your covers. It's not my fault that there's no market for them. If you're upset about losing money, why don't you raise hell with the companies you bought the covers from instead of taking it out on me? They've got your money, not me."

He didn't say a word.

"You can buy this stuff all over the place for less than a dollar. That's the reality of the market. I don't control the market, I just pay according to what it dictates. If your covers were in demand, I'd pay accordingly—but they're not. And I'm sure not going to take a lot of abuse over something I really don't want to buy. Your covers will be on their way back to you today."

"Maybe I was a little hasty," he said, his voice calmer. "It's just that I paid so much for the covers—it's a big shock to be told that they're worth next to nothing. I had no idea. I assumed that they would increase in value." His experience is one shared by most who've bought designer cover collections. Sadly, they should have investigated their resalability before buying.

He apologized for the outburst, and I shipped his covers back to him the same day. I am always amazed at how people "invest" in things without doing any homework. Perhaps I shouldn't be. After all, the time-honored adage holds: "A fool and his money are soon parted."

Don't expect to make a fortune buying mint new issues. Don't expect to make money on designer covers and other mass-marketed "collectibles." Buy them only if you enjoy them. And when it's time to cash out, don't blame the stamp dealer because your investment didn't turn out the way you thought it would.

Another common fallacy is that stamps derive value from age. I have mentioned this misconception elsewhere, however an incident at a dealer friend's store puts the whole issue nicely in perspective. Dealers get frequent inquiries about old stamps—especially used stamps—many of which are more than

100 years old. They're old, so they must be valuable, the reasoning goes. Most often, they're one-, two- or three-cent denominations. However, a century ago, before the advent of the telephone and other electronic communications, the bulk of personal and business communications was accomplished by letter. Used stamps of standard letter rates—one-, two- and three-cents—are abundant even today and have little individual value.

Nevertheless, the woman at my dealer friend's counter was adamant that her old stamps must be valuable. He tried vainly to explain to her that age alone did not determine a stamp's value. Try as he might, he couldn't seem to make her understand. She could not or would not grasp the principle of rarity and demand, retorting again and again, "But these stamps are more than a hundred years old!"

Finally, in desperation, he replied, "I have a two-billion-year-old rock in my back yard. How much is it worth?"

She thought for a moment, then a scowl crossed her face. Abruptly she turned on heel and walked out without another word. I chuckled. He had, indeed, put the situation in perspective.

While on the subject of myths, again and again dealers hear stories about sets of full sheets of 1893 Columbians and used inverted Jennies retrieved from wastebaskets. Experienced dealers take these stories with a grain of salt.

The myth of the used inverted Jenny persists. The original error sheet of 100 was broken up and the stamps sold to collectors. Each stamp from the original sheet is individually identifiable, and the current whereabouts of most are known.   The wife of an unfortunate collector—so the story goes—in search of a stamp to mail a bill, entered his study and used an inverted Jenny she found lying on his desk. Later, an alert collector retrieved the used Jenny from a wastebasket at the receiving end. It's just another philatelic myth. The truth is that no used copies of the inverted Jenny are known.

Then there are the Zeppelins of 1930. They were on sale for only a few weeks in the spring of 1930: in Washington, D.C. from April 19 through June 30, and in various other cities from April 21 through June 7. A fact not generally known is that they were not on sale in every post office throughout the nation. They were available only in a select number of large cities, typically not more than one or two per state. In Colorado, they were on sale only in Denver.

Nevertheless, you hear tales of complete sets of Zeppelin sheets set aside by phantom relatives, often said to be one-time postmasters of small towns out in the middle of nowhere. The teller will swear the story is true. The problem is that the town out in the middle of nowhere never received Zeppelins. To this day, enterprising individuals still scour small rural post offices in hopes of finding sets of long-forgotten Zeppelins—Zeppelins that were never there to begin with.

Speaking of Zeppelins, stamp dealers frequently hear the word "Zeppelin" mispronounced. The most common mispronunciation is "Zeffelin." That "f" sound grates against the ear of the *cognoscenti* like squeaky chalk on a blackboard.

There seems to be no limit to creative mispronunciation or misinformation. My favorite is the reply I received when I asked whether a collection contained any key airmails. The answer was "No, it doesn't have the inverted Zeffelin or anything like that." Just when you think you've heard it all, something new pops up. The inverted Zeffelin—it's got to be the ultimate rarity!

CULTURE SHOCK

Selling stamps is often a frustrating experience. It would be easier if everything were cut and dried, but the free market doesn't operate that way. The free market is a living, changing organism, which despite its vicissitudes, is perhaps the most efficient way of distributing goods and establishing values. The free market system is responsible for America's great abundance. Americans tend to take it for granted. They forget that free markets do not prevail in all parts of the world.

I recall the day Laszlo, a Hungarian exchange student, walked into Ron Hazard's stamp shop. It was back in the early 1970s. I was in the shop waiting to go to lunch with Ron when Laszlo walked in with a big, bright-red stockbook under his arm. He told us that he had recently arrived in the United States from Hungary to attend the University of Colorado for a year. His tuition and room and board were being paid, but he received no cash allowance, no spending money. In fact, he had been allowed to take only $10 in cash out of the country when he left Hungary.

"How can they expect you to get by on ten bucks—for an entire year?" I asked. College kids spend more than that on a date.

"Well, you see," he began, his English thick with an eastern European accent, "we are not allowed to export currency. Our country needs it for economic development. That is why I brought these stamps to America to sell. Although we are not permitted to bring cash, there is no restriction on stamps." He opened the large red stockbook. It bulged with bright, new, mint Hungarian stamps, neatly arranged row upon row, all of modest value.

Laszlo was a big, tall, likable fellow with a thick shock of blondish hair above his forehead and a smile a yard wide. He spoke enthusiastically of America, seemed excited to be here. At the same time, he seemed far more serious than American teenagers. His seriousness and his enthusiasm for America suddenly made me feel exquisitely lucky to be an American and sorry for those in the rest of the world who couldn't be. The three of us chatted for a while comparing philately in our respective countries.

"I would like to sell some of these stamps," Laszlo finally said. "Perhaps you would like to buy the whole book?" he added hopefully. "Tell me, what is your pleasure?"

Ron paged through the bright red stockbook. The stamps lay row on row, pretty and in perfect condition. The trouble was, he really didn't want the stamps, but neither did he want to hurt Laszlo's feelings. What is it about Americans that inclines them to want to be hospitable to foreigners?

Ron was on the spot. I knew he was trying to find a diplomatic way of saying no, a task made all the more difficult because Laszlo was such a likable fellow and because he was counting on the stamps to raise cash. "The stamps are very nice," Ron said at last, "but there's not much demand for Hungarian stamps in this part of the country."

"Well, you could take just a few then," Laszlo responded in a spirit of accommodation. "I can use whatever money I can get." Unfortunately, Ron did not want even a few. Not only was there no market locally for Hungarian stamps, but the market in general for recent Hungarian stamps was very poor. They were worth, perhaps, ten percent of catalogue value at best.

"Take what you like at seventy percent of catalogue value," Laszlo offered. I gasped silently—70 percent was far, far above retail price, let alone wholesale.

"Well, I don't think so," Ron replied uncomfortably.

"Ah, I see. The price must be negotiated," Laszlo said. "Well, I could reduce the price to sixty-six percent, but I can go no lower. That is less than I would get at the state store."

"The state store? What is the state store?"

"State stores are the only stamp stores permitted to sell stamps in my country. Private stores are not allowed. The state sets the buying and selling prices."

"How much would you get for these stamps at the state store," Ron asked.

"Seventy percent of the catalogue value," Laszlo replied.

"And collectors pay full catalogue value at the state store?"

"Yes, of course," Laszlo answered as if to say: "How could it be otherwise?"

"What if you wanted to sell stamps privately to another collector?"

"Well, private individuals are not permitted to sell stamps. Only trading is permitted. Buying and selling quantities of stamps is speculation. Speculation is not allowed in our socialist society," he said, then added reflexively, but unnecessarily, "I accumulated these for trading purposes."

The profit motive is universal, I thought, *despite the disclaimer.*

"In this country anyone can buy and sell stamps," Ron said.

"Ah, yes, it is wonderful," Laszlo said, nodding appreciatively.

"The open market determines prices," Ron continued. "The law of supply and demand. If a stamp is scarce and lots of buyers want it, its price rises. On the other hand, if few buyers want it, regardless of how scarce it is, its price falls. The stamp catalogue is only a guide. Stamps trade higher or lower than catalogue according to supply and demand. Do you understand?"

Laszlo nodded.

"Hungarian stamps—especially recent issues—trade at a fraction of catalogue because there are so few collectors for them in this country. Supply is abundant, demand weak. If I bought your stamps, they would sit on the shelf for a long, long time. I don't get requests for Hungarian stamps, so there's no incentive for me to tie up money in them. Do you follow?"

Again, Laszlo nodded.

"I can buy Hungarian stamps like yours at auction for about ten percent of catalogue value, twelve percent at most."

"Ten percent!" Laszlo exclaimed in astonishment. "How can that be? That is not even fair. These are good stamps. Excellent condition, like new." Dark clouds crossed his face. Ron looked uncomfortable. No one likes to be the bearer of bad news, but it was the truth.

"I know," Ron replied defensively. "I'm not suggesting that they're not good. I'm trying to explain to you how the free market works. I'm not making you an offer. I'm telling you how much the stamps would cost elsewhere. I can't pay you seventy percent for the same goods I can buy for ten percent elsewhere. My customers won't pay seventy percent, let alone the eighty percent or more I'd have to charge to make a profit if I paid your price. They'll buy from the cheapest source. That's how the free market works."

Laszlo frowned, did not appear convinced. *What kind of capitalist trick is this?* he must have wondered. But Ron wasn't trying to talk him out of his stamps—he didn't even want them. I knew that. And I knew he felt terrible about having to burst the young Hungarian's balloon.

"You can buy stamps like yours at full retail for less than you're asking," he said. Laszlo still looked doubtful. "It's the truth. Full retail. Way under seventy percent."

Laszlo rubbed his chin and scowled.

"Listen, why don't you try some of the local stamp clubs?" Ron suggested. "You'll get a better idea of the market, of stamp values. Won't he?" Ron said, turning to me.

"Yes." I nodded. "Good idea. You can sell or trade. Get a feel for the market. Meet a lot of nice people." It was a good idea, and Laszlo would discover that Ron wasn't a villain.

"Let me give you a list of clubs," Ron said, jotting down names.

The clubs would orient Laszlo to the American stamp market, and I had a feeling that he would rapidly become aware of the profit opportunities that existed. I could visualize him buying Hungarian stamps at auction in America for ten percent and selling them back home for 70 percent.

"Thank you," Laszlo said as Ron handed him the list. His hostility had ebbed. "I'm not sure I like this free market system too much."

"You will," I said, sure that in the long run he would find it pleasant and profitable. The bright side of the free market is that you can buy and sell to your heart's content. No need to deal surreptitiously, no need to worry about the police or an informant snooping in your business, and no need to keep a watchful eye over your shoulder. No limitation is placed on enterprise.

"Come back and see me after you've been to a few club meetings," Ron said.

"Okay," Laszlo said as he left. "And thank you." The smile was back on his face. I had a hunch that Laszlo would do very well in the free market.

What Laszlo learned that day was a fundamental fact of economic life in the America—stamp values are determined by the free market, not by the state, and not by catalogues.

IT'S A TWO WAY STREET

As Laszlo learned, economic customs vary from country to country. I, too, learned that lesson the hard way. I learned that even in western nations surprises await the unsuspecting.

As a dealer, I'm ever alert for ways to maximize profits. A few years back, I acquired a specialized collection of German flight covers, the kind of material for which there is little market locally. So I sent it to New York, curious to see what kind of offers might be forthcoming.

The best offer I could get was $2,500. It was not a bad price, but by virtue of the collection's specialized, esoteric nature, I felt it should be worth considerably more—especially to the right buyer. I got to thinking that Germany might be the best market. Foreign auctions often yield top prices for highly specialized material, so I packed it up and sent it off to a major German auction firm with a request for an estimate of what it would realize at unreserved sale.

I was both delighted and astounded when I received their estimate of $5,000 accompanied by an advance of $2,500. The advance was subject to fairly hefty interest but that didn't bother me because $2,500 was as much as I had been offered for the entire lot in New York.

I found the German consignment forms far more complex than those typically used by American auction firms, but I didn't think much of it at the time. Having been to Germany, I was familiar with the German penchant for detail and precision, and assumed that the consignment forms, while complex, were merely routine. I waded through several pages of German microtype—translating as best I could with my superficial knowledge of German—then signed and returned them.

I sent a letter along with the forms inquiring about when the covers would be offered. The Germans replied that it would be several months hence. They explained that their next auction already contained quite a bit of the same type of material and that too much of the same thing would hurt prices. *Very shrewd*, I thought. *Very professional. Nothing like German precision.*

When, after a few months, I had heard nothing from Germany, I called. I asked for the director, the title below the signature on the cover letter I had received months before. His English was excellent, but his accent, thick as molasses.

"Ah, yes, Herr Datz, we have your covers," he said. "Do not be concerned, they will be in the next auction. We will get very good prices. I know you will be pleased." I wasn't really concerned, just anxious to liquidate the lot and be paid. I was glad to hear that the covers would be sold soon. As we chatted, I mentioned the terms once again, just for my own peace of mind. I wanted to make sure that everything would be sold.

"No reserves," I reiterated. "I want to sell everything. I don't care what price it brings." Since the estimate had been so liberal, I really didn't care if the lot sold for less; even $4,500 or $3,500 would have been okay. As far as I was concerned, anything above $2,500 was found money. "Do you understand?" I stressed.

"Do not worry, Herr Datz. You will get good prices. I guarantee it. We will handle everything to your satisfaction," he assured me. So I didn't worry. I just waited.

At length I received a copy of the auction catalogue along with a list of my lots. The catalogue was superb, the Mercedes-Benz of auction catalogues. I felt silly about ever having worried. I could hear that German voice counseling wisely: "Be patient, Herr Datz. These things take time." *Yes,* I thought, *perhaps we Americans are too impetuous.*

Soon after the sale, I received a registered package containing prices realized and—to my surprise—the most of my covers. There was no check. The covers that had actually sold realized tremendous prices. The problem was that only a few choice, key pieces had sold; the rest had been returned. The items sold amounted to only $1,100. To make matters worse, the auction requested that I remit the difference between the $1,100 net and their $2,500 advance: $1,400. Since the advance had been drawn in Deutsche marks, the Germans expected a refund in marks. In the months since I had received the advance, the German mark had advanced against the dollar, so the refund, including interest, was going to cost quite a bit more than the simple $1,400 difference.

More than a little annoyed, I got on the telephone to Germany. "I told you to sell all the covers," I complained angrily. "Remember?—no reserves! I told you I didn't care what prices they sold for."

"That is correct, Herr Datz," the German replied precisely, coolly, his voice completely unruffled. "And we noted that on your records. Perhaps you did not understand the policy of this firm. We cannot permit an item to sell for less than we think it should be worth. That would only encourage bidders to think that they could make low bids on everything. That would not be good for the market. After all, it is our responsibility to maintain an orderly market. It was all explained in the forms we sent you. You did read them, did you not, Herr Datz?"

At last, I understood. They protected all lots with reserves so that bidders would not become accustomed to buying too cheaply. The consignor could request minimums or waive them, however, his actions had no effect on house-imposed minimums. I had scanned the forms, relying on my imperfect knowledge of German, and assumed that their terms and conditions were similar to those of American auctions. I made a big mistake by assuming too much.

I sent the refund to Germany, then shipped the unsold covers to New York. I received $1,500 for the balance, which when added to the $1,100 I had received from Germany, amounted to $2,500. After deducting interest, phone calls and arbitrage, the final figure amounted to a few hundred dollars less than the $2,500 cash I could have had all those months earlier.

I learned the hard way that business policies and customs differ from country to country. One can take nothing for granted. When dealing overseas—especially in a foreign language—be very careful to understand the terms and conditions before doing business. And get a competent translation before signing anything!

FRIENDLY PERSUASION

The man who entered my office carrying a heavy carton full of stamp albums introduced himself as Bill Shannon. He appeared to be in his early thirties. His grip was firm and his voice, businesslike. He explained that his father had died some months earlier leaving a rather substantial collection, which he now wanted to sell. From that first moment, Bill Shannon impressed me as a man who knew exactly what he wanted.

I invited him to have a seat. He took a chair in front of my desk and placed the carton of albums on the floor at his side rather than on my desk. It seemed to me that he wanted to establish the ground rules before the first album was ever opened.

"My father built a large collection," he said. "I know it's worth a lot of money. He collected diligently all his adult life—for as long as I can remember—and he was very serious about it." If the elder Shannon had been anything like his son, then indeed, he had been a serious man.

"Neither my brother nor I are interested in stamps," he continued. "We'd prefer to have the money, providing we can get a good price. I would like your offer for the collection. But I want you to know that I intend to get other offers," he cautioned. "I don't know much about stamps, so it's the only way I know to protect myself. Nothing personal, just prudent business. You understand, I'm sure. I've brought a sampling, a group of albums from various countries. I'd like you to figure each country separately because I plan to keep some of them." He had laid out his strategy as neatly as stamps arranged on the pages of an award-winning exhibit.

"I appreciate your directness," I replied, "so I too will be direct. I don't charge to make an offer, but I do charge for an appraisal. I've spent far too many hours valuing collections only to have people thank me and leave, saying they'll think it over. Unfortunately, I simply can't afford to make appraisals for nothing." He looked at me calmly and said nothing. I had the impression he was studying me.

"As I said, I don't charge to make an offer, but the seller's got to be serious about selling. I want to feel confidant that we will do business if my offer is reasonable. Then I'm willing to risk my time. I think that's only fair." Shannon nodded as I spoke. "And it's my policy to make an offer on an entire collection, not stamp by stamp or section by section. It's just too time-consuming to try to negotiate stamp by stamp, section by section."

"I'm serious about selling," he replied. "But I'm not going to commit in advance to take your offer just because you've invested time to make it. And I do want to know the value of each album," he said, his voice precise and to the point. He had known long before coming through my front door exactly how he wanted to do business. I sensed that he was not about to change his mind.

His goals and mine differed but there was nothing to be gained by being confrontational. "Let me take a quick look through the albums you've brought in," I suggested, "just to see if they're of interest. I'll know right away if the matter is worth pursuing."

"Okay," he said.

The first volume contained specialized France. I riffled the pages. The classic period was sparse but the twentieth century looked fairly complete: commemoratives, definitives, semi-postals, airmails, plus the first three souvenir sheets—virtually all mint and in mounts. Definitely a quality collection, far superior to most.

I paged through a second time more slowly. Stamp mounts are a good sign that a collector is quality conscious. A random check revealed that most stamps were never hinged. Bill Shannon's father had been a meticulous individual. He'd put together a beautiful collection worth serious money.

"Very nice," I said, reaching for the next album. He had stacked the remaining albums on my desk while I'd looked at the French collection. It was the same story, album after album. Some of the other countries weren't as complete as the French collection, but each contained an abundance of quality material.

"Impressive," I said. "I can see that your father was a serious collector. How many more do you have?"

"Dozens and dozens. Dad seemed to have an album for just about every country. Some have more stamps than others. He concentrated on certain areas—Germany, British Commonwealth, Scandinavia."

The areas he mentioned happened to be among the most desirable and most salable ones. I knew from experience that collections of such scope and quality were few and far between.

"If the rest of it's as nice as what I've just seen, we're talking about a substantial sum," I said. Shannon allowed the faintest hint of a smile, as if pleased to hear his expectation confirmed. "I'd like to buy it. The question is, are you ready to sell?"

"Yes," he said, "but as I've explained, I know nothing about stamp values. I want to get several offers in order to satisfy myself that I have taken every reasonable measure to get the best price. That's the way my father would have gone about it so that's the way I'm going about it. You're the first dealer I've contacted. I'm learning as I go."

No dealer likes to be the first one to make an offer. "The collection's going to require a fair amount of time to do it justice. Suppose I take the time to make a thorough evaluation and offer—for the sake of argument—twenty-five thousand dollars. Then the next dealer riffles through it and says it looks like it's worth at least twenty thousand, a figure somewhat less than he's really willing to pay. It's a starting price, a price to test the waters. Your reaction is immediate, reflexive and indignant: 'I've already been offered twenty-five thousand!' That's just what he wants to hear. Now he knows exactly what he's up against.

"Then he'll flip through the albums again more slowly saying, 'Let me take another look. I may have missed something.' Then while he's looking, he'll ask skeptically, 'Who offered twenty-five thousand?' You'll respond defensively and give my name to prove the credibility of your assertion. He'll know then how much you've been offered and by whom.

"Most dealers are familiar with each other's buying habits, so he knows that if I'm willing to pay twenty-five thousand, he can pay that much plus just enough more to clinch the deal. Next he says, 'I really haven't gone through it in detail, but the other offer sounds fair. I could really use the collection, so tell you what I'll do. I'll save you a trip back across town—I'll meet his offer and throw in a little something extra for your trouble. How does twenty-five thousand two-fifty sound?' And more often than not, you'll take it. I'll have done all the work and lose out to a two-hundred-and-fifty-dollar bump. That concerns me, Mr. Shannon. Not too long ago, I lost a collection for which I had offered ten thousand dollars by a hundred dollar bump. I have absolutely no problem with you getting other offers, but the thought of doing all the work and then getting bumped for a few dollars bothers me."

"I, too, appreciate directness," Shannon replied. "That's the way I like to do business. I can't guarantee I'll take your offer, but I will promise not to reveal it to another dealer or accept a marginally higher offer without letting you know first. I'm not going to pull the rug out from under you for a few bucks. I don't play games," he said, looking me straight in the eye. I believed him.

And so, because of the size and scope of the collection, and because I felt I could trust Bill Shannon, I did something I rarely do. I agreed to evaluate it without an appraisal fee.

Bill Shannon brought albums in once a week, a carton at a time. Seldom had I enjoyed working with a collection so much. The roll call of countries was impressive: the United States, Germany, Switzerland, the Netherlands, Scandinavia, France, Monaco, Austria, Spain, Belgium, Luxembourg, Liechtenstein, Andorra, Central and South America, Asia, Africa, and virtually every British Commonwealth country. The elder Shannon had faithfully purchased new issues over the decades and had worked backward to fill out the collections as well, acquiring numerous desirable mint sets of the 1920s, 1930s and 1940s. By the time I finished, I had more than 40 pages of figures on my yellow legal pad.

Each week, just like clockwork, Bill Shannon brought another carton of albums and picked up the one left the previous week. And each time, we spent an hour or so chatting. As the weeks passed, I got to know him. I was surprised to learn he was a bailbondsman, a man who made his living bailing criminals out of jail. That intrigued me.

"It must be exciting," I said, "working with all those murderers, thieves, rapists, and drug dealers."

He laughed. "It's neither as exciting nor as dangerous as you might think. Most of my business comes from drunk drivers, traffic offenders, and the like. Just ordinary people with homes and jobs who suddenly find themselves in jail and who will probably never be there again. I don't get involved with the high risk, violent criminal types. Actually, murderers are not really the worst risks for bail."

His comment surprised me. "What could be worse?" I asked.

"Con men—without question."

"Con men?" I repeated, thinking that they didn't sound particularly dangerous.

"Absolutely. Con men are born liars. They'll say anything to accomplish their purpose, be it to con someone out of money, get out of jail, plead for a reduced sentence, or whatever. They'll tell you whatever they think you want to hear. They're highly intelligent, very inventive, very creative. They're masters of verbal illusion. They have an intuitive understanding of human psychology, and they play on it like a virtuoso violinist.

"Con men believe they're more intelligent than other people. They're born actors, highly skillful. They create illusions in which they play out a part. The illusions blur with reality—they're like children playing pretend. That's what makes them so convincing.

"They're contemptuous of laws and regulations. They believe that laws don't apply to them. I think they actually live in a different world, a different reality. They get enormous pleasure and satisfaction from conning people, putting something over on them. It's a game to them, a game in which they prove their superiority by fooling others. From a bondsman's point of view, con men are the very worst risks because they'll tell you anything to get out of jail, then jump bail in the blink of an eye. You simply can't rely on anything they say."

I was fascinated.

"Most people think of criminals as mean and ugly, easy to recognize and avoid. But con men are the most charming, likable fellows you would ever want to meet. Their success is due to their ability to make people genuinely like them and trust them. Without tremendous charm, they'd get nowhere."

I had never thought about it before, but it made sense. No one likes or trusts a mean, nasty person, but a nice guy is naturally liked and trusted.

"Victims are always amazed that their trust has been betrayed. Often they won't even admit to themselves that they've misjudged a con man. Time and time again I've heard, 'He was the nicest man you'd ever want to meet. Why, he'd give you the shirt right off his back.' I could entertain you all afternoon with stories about their antics." And he did.

I found one story particularly amusing, although I'm sure the victim was not amused.

"The con man answered an ad to house-sit a college professor's home one summer," Shannon related. "The professor planned to spend several months abroad. The con man showed up, a hail fellow, well met. The professor liked him immediately. He gave him the job and left for the summer. No sooner did the con man move in than he assumed the professor's identity. He re-landscaped the house to his own taste. He ordered trees and rocks and even put in a lily pond. Then he redecorated the interior and threw lavish parties, charging the catering expenses to an account he had opened in the professor's name.

"He called all over the world on the professor's phone. Ran up enormous phone bills, stalled payment for months until the phone company finally disconnected him. But he didn't let that stop him. He intercepted a telephone repairman who had come to disconnect a neighbor's phone across the street. The neighbor had moved. Impersonating the neighbor, he told the repairman that he'd only moved across the street, and the phone should be reconnected there. The repairman obliged him, and the con man was back in business. He continued to run up phone bills until the ruse was discovered and the service disconnected.

"He ordered all kinds of merchandise delivered to the home, all of it charged to accounts he had opened impersonating the professor. Now mind you, he wasn't necessarily making money on all these transactions, he just enjoyed the con. He couldn't resist the opportunity to fool someone. He couldn't resist seeing what he could get away with. He even told the principal of the local high school that he would build a swimming pool for the school if the school would give his youngster help with a remedial course. And the principal believed him!"

I chuckled. It all sounded so absurd. The thought of a private citizen building a swimming pool for a school in return for some remedial help. How could anyone fall for that?

"When the professor finally returned from abroad, he found a home that he didn't recognize and a bunch of angry creditors. The con man was long gone by then, highly amused by the mischief he had caused. It was all a great and glorious joke—first rate fun!

"The con man related this story to me with great relish. He took great pride in his skill at conning people. I asked him why he had done it. He replied that when he got a clever idea, he just had to see if he could get away with it. He felt compelled to exploit every opportunity. He just couldn't resist. And you know, he was so charming you couldn't help but like him. Con men are like that—likable as hell. But the minute you trust them, they'll take advantage of you."

I looked forward to our weekly meetings, both for the stamps and the stories. Bill Shannon had met a lot of marvelous, wacky, Runyonesque characters during the course of his career, the kind most of us will never meet. And over the weeks, he shared his experiences with me.

Eight or ten weeks later, after the last batch of albums had been evaluated, it was time to make an offer. I wanted the collection badly, so I stretched to the limit. Bill Shannon thanked me for the offer and assured me that he'd let me know before accepting any other offer.

And in time, I did hear from him. He told me that none of the other dealers had spent as much time on the collection as I had or had displayed as much patience. I bought the bulk of the collection. He kept part of it, as he said he would, for sentimental reasons. The time I'd invested in it turned out to be time well spent. Bill Shannon and I have remained friends over the years, and whenever we get together, he never fails to entertain me with new stories about the characters he has met.

The way in which Bill Shannon approached the task of selling illustrates several points worth remembering. 1) It never hurts to get more than one offer. 2) It pays to be direct and straightforward. Put your cards on the table. Your directness will impress whomever you're dealing with. 3) Establish a rapport with a dealer if possible. Not only will it make your transaction more pleasant, but potentially more profitable as well.

HOME ON THE RANGE

I had misgivings as I made the 100-mile drive from Denver to Cheyenne, Wyoming. Except for the appraisal fee, I was sure the trip would turn out to be a waste of time and turn up just another routine collection of U.S. singles and plate blocks from 1945 to date. Don't get me wrong; there's nothing wrong with U.S. stamps from 1945 to date. It's just that there's not enough profit potential in that type of collection to justify a 100-mile drive.

I was on the road because a trust officer at the Cattleman's National Bank of Cheyenne had called requesting an estate appraisal. He knew nothing about stamps, so he couldn't describe the collection meaningfully except to say that it consisted of four volumes of U.S. stamps.

I advised the banker that my minimum appraisal fee was $50 if he brought the stamps to my office in Denver or $100 if I traveled to Cheyenne. He preferred that I come to Cheyenne.

My misgivings about finding any meaningful stamps in Cheyenne were due to my only previous philatelic experience in that city. In the early 1980s, Cheyenne hosted its first stamp show—CHYPEX, short for Cheyenne Philatelic Exhibition. CHYPEX was a three-day show held in early September at a brand new shopping mall.

On the east and west coasts, mall shows have a reputation for being rinky-dink affairs, but not so in the heartland. There the attitude is more informal and neighborly, the atmosphere more like a rural county fair than a big city convention. You pitch in and help promote. You meet people, make new friends, do some business, and have a good time. At the time, the population of Cheyenne was only about 50,000.

The moment I arrived at the mall it became apparent just how informal an affair CHYPEX was. I had no trouble finding a parking place—the parking lot was deserted. I parked directly in front of the main entrance. Moving in was a snap. It was only a short distance from my parking place to the front door and just a few steps inside to the large open space where the show had been set up.

I was among the first to arrive. The bare, vacant dealers' tables reminded me of circled wagons. None were marked with dealer assignments so I had no clue as to who belonged where, and the show chairman was nowhere to be found.

"Which space is mine?" I asked after I finally managed to locate him ten minutes later on the other side of the cavernous mall.

"Oh, take any one you want," he replied offhandedly.

"No assigned tables?" I asked, not believing my ears.

"Nope," he replied. "First come, first served. Set up wherever you like." That was odd, indeed, because bourse spaces are always assigned, but apparently he was unaware of that custom. *What a refreshing contrast from New York, Chicago and Los Angeles,* I thought. No waiting at registration tables for IDs. No worrying about where your space was located. No hassles trying to find parking or unload. No $10 tips to lethargic union stewards to expedite setup. I had a feeling I was going to like Cheyenne. I chose the table directly inside the main entrance—front and center. I could see my car just outside the door, only a short distance away. There were only a few other cars in the lot, still it was early.

I unpacked a stack of mint sheets from an accumulation I'd purchased a few weeks earlier. They were mostly post-1945 three-cent commemoratives, which I sold at face value in order to get people to stop at my table and browse. Collectors find it impossible to resist the urge to rummage through a pile of old mint sheets.

"Not those mint sheets again," groaned John Lord, who was setting up nearby and who retailed similar mint sheets at face value plus ten percent. He started to complain about how my face value offerings had killed his mint sheet business at the last show.

"What discount will you give me if I buy the whole lot?" he asked.

"Face minus five percent if you take them all."

"Deal," he said, obviously pleased that he just eliminated the competition. The stack came to about $300. He wrote out a check and hurried off to his table. The show would be opening soon.

Ten o'clock—the official opening time—rolled around without a single collector in evidence, not one. In fact, the mall itself was largely deserted. Precious few shoppers strolled its broad central walkway. An optimist by nature, I assumed things would pick up in their own good time. Perhaps the announced opening time had been misstated. Perhaps the show was supposed to open at eleven o'clock instead of ten. And it was Friday morning. Fridays can be slow.

Eleven o'clock rolled around and still not a single collector had appeared. Odd indeed. Dealers were beginning to make nervous jokes such as "What if they gave a stamp show and nobody came?" The only activity at the bourse tables consisted of dealers perusing each other's stock and doing business among themselves.

By noon the dealers had formed a pool; whoever made the first retail sale would win. You may think I'm exaggerating, but I'm not. This is a factual account—there were simply no retail customers. I began to wonder if there were any stamp collectors in Cheyenne. The evidence appeared to indicate that there were not. The mall was as dead as a deserted street at three o'clock in the morning. Where were all the people? Very strange indeed.

It began to remind me of something out of the TV show *The Twilight Zone*. I visualized Rod Serling standing in one of the shop doorways just out of sight, cigarette in hand, introducing an unseen audience to this episode, "You see before you stamp dealers gathered for a routine show. They have readied their wares in anticipation of the customers they soon expect. But no customers will be forthcoming. You see, these stamp dealers think they're at CHYPEX. What they don't know, but will soon discover to their dismay, is that they have set up shop in a strange desolate place, a place known as the Twilight Zone." Bring up theme music, dissolve shot of Serling, and into action.

Back in the real world, one o'clock came and went and still not a single retail customer had appeared. Then, just after two o'clock, a shout went up. Someone had just made the first retail sale of the day. Everyone craned their necks to see who the lucky dealer was. The customer was a middle-aged woman wearing a nondescript, brown coat. After she finished at the first dealer, she slowly worked her way around the remaining tables, pausing at each to see what might interest her. The dealers watched her anxiously, like cats watching a bird. But, disappointingly, she made no other purchases.

As the afternoon wore on, a few more people showed up, but not many. And Saturday was almost as bad. By Saturday evening, my retail sales amounted to slightly more than $100—my worst show ever. Of course, I had the $300 from the mint sheet sale, which turned out to be the big deal of the show. Unfortunately, John Lord's coup had backfired—there were no customers for his mint sheets. They sat neatly stacked on his table awaiting buyers that never materialized. There was just no traffic at CHYPEX or in the mall. I wondered how the mall stayed in business. I packed up Saturday evening and didn't bother to return Sunday. CHYPEX was the slowest show I had ever attended. As far as I know, there has never been a CHYPEX II.

My earlier experience at CHYPEX made me doubt that anything significant waited to be found at the bank in Cheyenne. I resigned myself to making a routine appraisal and driving 100 miles back to Denver.

Soon I arrived in Cheyenne. Pickup trucks, blue jeans, cowboy boots and western hats give downtown Cheyenne an informal appearance, more like the main street of small town than a state capital. I found a parking place right in front of the bank. Several were available. I dropped a quarter in the parking meter and went inside the bank.

The trust officer was pleasant but reserved. He ushered me into a plain, completely spartan conference room. Four diminutive albums—the size of grammar school theme books—lay stacked in the middle of a conference table large enough to have been the deck of an aircraft carrier.

"The heirs would like to know the current market value of the collection," the trust officer said, motioning toward the albums. He seated himself across from me, and during the entire time I was there, never once spoke unless first addressed. I took out a legal pad and began. The room was absolutely still. I felt like a student taking an exam under the watchful eye of a stern professor.

The first album contained mint blocks spanning the years 1940 to 1952, all carefully arranged on quadrille pages. Its only highlight, a set of famous Americans. Just as I had expected, it was a very modest collection. I noted its value on the legal pad and thought to myself: *Three albums to go. I'll be out of here in ten minutes.*

The second album, however, stopped me dead in my tracks. It contained a run of used U.S. singles from the first issue in 1847 onward. And it was more or less complete, page after page: 1861s, 1869s, banknotes, first Bureau issues of 1894, and so on, right up through the Presidential series. No short sets, and few faults. I checked the stamps page by page, astounded by the level of quality. Nineteenth century material is notoriously defective, but these stamps were uniformly select.

The collection had been formed by a discriminating individual. The stamps were mounted on clean white quadrille pages—no borders, no lines. An elegant presentation, like works of fine art on crisp chalk-white gallery walls. Occasionally, used blocks of four or more—such as gorgeous examples of $2 and $5 Franklins of 1918—lay interspersed among the singles. The album was loaded with breathtaking stamps.

The third album contained mint commemoratives complete from the Columbians onward both as singles and in blocks of four, except for the dollar value Columbian and Trans-Mississippi issues, which were represented by single stamps only. Airmails, too, were complete, including blocks of four for all issues except the Zeppelins, present only in single copies. The blocks were uniformly fresh and well centered, their colors bright and rich, kept fresh and vivid by years of storage away from light in the bone-dry Wyoming air. And the perforations on the blocks marched arrow-straight and true down the wide spaces between the stamps. The effect was stunning. Never before had I seen so many pristine stamps in one place.

The fourth album contained mint definitives—both singles and blocks of four, complete from the Washington-Franklins onward except for blocks of the rare blue papers. Stocksheets at the back of the album contained a dazzling number of fresh, never-hinged duplicates. I felt as if I'd stumbled into the treasure-laden tomb of an Egyptian pharaoh.

I paged through the albums a second time slowly, calculating values as I went. Then I went through a third time. Each time, I was more impressed. When at last I finished, two hours had elapsed, although it seemed like no more than ten minutes.

I couldn't get over the quality. Like all dealers, I was used to seeing mediocre run-of-the-mill collections, collections filled with seconds, collections with more spaces than stamps. The collection in front of me was a treat to be savored.

"First rate," I said. "And valuable."

"I thought it would be," the banker said. "It belonged to the man who founded the bank. He was an avid stamp collector. He died in 1952. The collection belongs to his children." That explained why the collection ended in 1952. He would have been in his prime during the 1910s and 1920s. No wonder the collection contained so many exceptional stamps from that era. It was apparent from the album pages that he had been a no-nonsense man. He had concentrated on completion in the highest quality obtainable. No pack-rat hoard, no jumbles of duplicates. Just the best possible example of each stamp mounted simply, modestly on white quadrille pages. Nothing extraneous to distract from their beauty. They stood entirely on their own merits, a testament to a man who appreciated quality, but found no need to flaunt it.

"Is the collection for sale?"

"I don't know," the trust officer replied. "That will be up to the heirs. I'll report your evaluation, but the decision is theirs. I really don't know what they have in mind." Then, "You mentioned auction on the phone. How does that work?"

I gave him an overview and suggested that because the collection contained so many scarce, high-quality stamps, auction would likely yield the best result—probably in the neighborhood of $30,000. I further explained that my cash price for outright purchase would be 30 percent less than the estimated auction realization. He nodded knowingly. Bankers seem to have a special appreciation for the value of cash in hand. I reminded him that the appraisal fee was refundable in the event we did business.

"Write up the appraisal and send an invoice for your fee. I'll let you know what the heirs decide," he said in conclusion.

Upon my return to Denver, I sent the formal appraisal. In due course, I received a check for the fee. Weeks passed. I had nearly forgotten about the collection when the banker called.

"They have decided to take your cash offer, if it's still open," he said.

"It's open," I said, surprised that they had decided to sell rather than consign to auction and delighted at the opportunity to buy it.

"When can you come up and get it?" he asked.

"How about tomorrow morning?" I said, half worried that they might change their minds in the meantime. "I can be there by ten. And by the way, do you want a cashier's check?"

"That's not necessary," he said. "Your business check will be just fine. I'll be expecting you at ten o'clock."

When I arrived the next morning, the banker introduced me to an elderly gentleman, one of the heirs. He appeared to be in his seventies or eighties, but his grip was firm. He looked more like a ranch hand—western shirt, denim jeans, and cowboy boots—than heir to a substantial estate. We moved to the boardroom, and while the banker readied the papers, we chatted. Curious, I asked the old gentlemen, "Why did you decide to sell the collection rather than auction it?"

"Well, at my age you don't like to wait around for your money," he replied with a grin. "The stamps weren't doing much good gathering dust in the closet. We'd forgotten all about them until Lucy—she was my sister—died and we had to clean out her house."

It's fascinating what happens to stamp collections. A wonderful collection lying forgotten in a closet for years.

"Didn't you know they were valuable?" I asked.

"Well, it's like this. When Dad died, we were pretty busy parceling out the land, the cattle, and the oil. We gave the stamps to Lucy, thought she might like to fiddle with 'em. But I guess she just put 'em up in the closet and forgot about 'em," he said matter-of-factly.

His words reminded me that Wyoming was a rough, weathered kind of place populated by a no-nonsense breed of people who had retained the same sense of fundamental values held by their pioneer forebears. They appreciated down-to-earth things like land, cattle, and oil—they didn't give stamps a second thought.

"None of us are getting any younger, so I figured we might as well turn 'em into cash. Besides, your appraisal was so much higher than that other one."

I wasn't aware that they had gotten a second opinion, but I was pleased that my estimate was higher. "How much was the other appraisal, if you don't mind my asking?"

"Five thousand dollars," he replied. The figure stunned me. I couldn't believe that any competent dealer could underestimate a collection so severely.

"Your offer was real generous. Why, I would have sold you the collection for $6,000 in a minute and been glad to get it," he said with a twinkle in his eye. I got the impression that he thought he'd just made a very clever deal, but his good humored self-satisfaction didn't bother me. My philosophy is that offering the best possible price always pays off in the long run—you buy more collections. And I was thrilled to have this one. However, one thing puzzled me. Who had made the ridiculously low appraisal?

"I'd be very interested to know who made the other appraisal," I said.

"Don't recall offhand," he replied, rubbing his chin thoughtfully. "We found the appraisal paper with the collection. It was done right after Dad died, back in '52. Who would have thought those old stamps would be worth so much more today?"

The appraisal had been done 30 years before!

The banker had the bill of sale ready and the old gentleman signed it. I handed him my check. We shook hands. I tucked the four slim albums under my arm and departed, happy that the mystery of the low offer had been explained. It had bothered me to think that a dealer would intentionally make such a ridiculously low offer.

During the drive back to Denver, the stamps rested on the front seat next to me. The limitless, high prairie stretched like a brown sea to the horizon, and the words of the anthem of that part of the world strayed into my consciousness . . . *Home, home on the range . . . where the deer and the antelope play . . . where seldom is heard a discouraging word . . . and the skies are not cloudy all day.* The old man's words too milled persistently, like restless cattle, around and around in my brain: *Six thousand dollars would have bought the collection . . . land, cattle, and oil . . . we thought Lucy might like to fiddle with 'em.* What a morning it had been!

GREAT EXPECTATIONS

In my mind, June is the most pleasant month of the year. Spring—raw and predictable—has at last ripened into early summer, fresh and bright and full of promise.

The young lady seated across the desk from me reminded me of a June day. She was also fresh and bright and full of promise. Her name was Dorothy Winchester, and her family had assembled in my office to sell their stamps. The Winchesters were dryland farmers who made their home on the high plains in the winter wheat country east of Denver.

Mr. Winchester had called about the stamps a few days earlier. His daughter, Dorothy, had just graduated from high school, and he wanted to sell Grandpa's stamps to finance her college education.

Seated across from me, the Winchester clan looked like a Norman Rockwell painting, a family portrait straight out of the heartland—honest, hardworking folks dressed up in their Sunday best, clean and pressed but vaguely out of fashion. Mr. Winchester sat in the center chair, Mrs. Winchester on his right, and Dorothy on his left. Three other children, two boys and a girl—ranging in age from perhaps eight to fifteen—stood behind them, neatly scrubbed and dressed as if it were the first day of school.

Dorothy seemed an appropriate name, I thought, because she bore a striking resemblance to the Dorothy of *Wizard of OZ* fame. I could picture her strolling down the Yellow Brick Road.

"Grandpa told us to hang onto the stamps, that one day we could send the kids to college on them," Mr. Winchester explained. His voice was as plain and unpretentious as the flat brown rangeland where he made his home. "Grandpa's been gone for a number of years now. Dorothy's just out of high school and ready for college, so the time has come to sell. I don't know the first thing about stamps. I've got no idea what they're worth, other than Grandpa said we could send the kids to college on them."

I hoped that we would all be pleasantly surprised. Dryland farmers tend to be the ultimate inconspicuous consumers. Having been raised in rural Colorado, I knew farmers who wore bib overalls wherever they went, always had mud on their boots, and drove 15-year-old pickup trucks, yet were worth millions. They never let on about their wealth, so people tended to underestimate them. The Winchester collection could be a real sleeper, I thought, recalling the Cheyenne bank collection.

As he spoke, Mr. Winchester produced a cigar box and placed it on my desk. I opened it and looked through it. It contained an assortment of utterly common used stamps from the 1930s, stamps torn off envelopes and tucked away in the box. Here and there a few mint commemoratives peeked out. The entire contents were not worth even five dollars.

"Is this the entire collection?" I asked, hoping desperately that he would say no and pull out the good stuff.

"Yup, that's it," he replied.

Suddenly I felt very uncomfortable. For all practical purposes, the stamps were worthless. Normally I would have explained the facts, thanked them for coming in, and then gotten on with my business. Now, however, I would have to tell this family that the treasure they were counting on to send Dorothy to college was worthless. When they learned the truth, more than college dreams would be shattered—Grandpa would be exposed as a hoaxer.

The Winchester family—serious, humble, trusting folks—held me in their collective gaze, waiting expectantly. I wondered why Grandpa had told them such a tale? Had he really believed the stamps would send the kids to college someday? Had he made the remark lightly in passing? Was it an innocent exaggeration that had been misinterpreted? Or was he simply a fool? Did he have any idea of the effect his thoughtless remark would later have on his family? These troubling thoughts passed through my mind in the brief moment before I had to break the bad news.

The Winchesters waited silently. Dorothy was smiling; she looked immensely pleased. Her hands lay neatly folded in her lap. The joy of high school graduation and the anticipation of college must have been light in her heart. It occurred to me that Dorothy was probably the first one in her family to have the chance to go to college. *Grandpa—what a fool,* I thought to myself. How could anyone do this to their family?

Then, suddenly, I realized that the Winchesters were not among the well-to-do farmers. They really were counting on the stamps to send Dorothy to college. Grandpa had told them that the cigar box contained a treasure, and all these years, they had clung to that belief. The small cigar box, in fact, contained their dreams. Unfortunately, Grandpa had lied. The cigar box was a cruel hoax. It would not take Dorothy down the Yellow Brick Road to a better, brighter future.

I closed the lid carefully and pushed the box back across the desk toward them. "I'm afraid I have some bad news for you," I began. "I want you to understand that I'm not making an offer to buy your stamps, but I want to let you know what they're worth just the same. The reason I'm not making an offer is because I don't want you to think that I'm understating the value of the box in order to buy it cheaply. The entire box is worth only about five dollars." The bombshell dropped. The Winchesters were absolutely stunned—blank-faced, drop-jawed stunned.

"Dad told us these stamps would be valuable someday," Mrs. Winchester said. "Are you sure you're not mistaken?"

"I wish I were. Unfortunately, they're very common. That's why I told you that I wasn't making an offer. I really can't use them nor are you likely to find anyone else who will give you much for them. My guess is that if you shop them around, you can expect offers of about five dollars. I'm sorry I couldn't have given you better news. Are you sure there aren't some other stamps at home? Perhaps they were the ones your father referred to," I suggested.

"No. This is everything," Mrs. Winchester replied, shaking her head. Their smiles had vanished, replaced by grimness. Dorothy fidgeted and Mr. Winchester reached for the cigar box.

"Thank you for your time," he said stoically, in the firm, quiet voice of a man who knows how to meet adversity head-on without showing emotion. I admired him.

"I'm sorry they weren't worth more," I said again, genuinely sorry.

"That's okay. It's not your fault," he said, reaching across the desk to shake my hand. Then the Winchester family trooped out. *What a damn fool Grandpa was,* I thought again. He should have kept his mouth shut.

Stamp dealers hear similar sad stories again and again, of foolish exaggerations planted by unthinking relatives. If only they knew the heartache they caused. Did Dorothy go to college? I don't know. But every time I recall the incident, I hope that she was able to find a way.

An innocent remark, a boast about the value of a collection to a member of the family, all too often turns into a nightmarish briar-patch through which seller and dealer alike must struggle. Those who mislead usually do so inadvertently. It's only human nature to boast, to exaggerate the value of one's stamps and revel in the imaginary wealth. It seems harmless enough. Only later, when heirs try to sort fact from fantasy, does misinformation work its mischief. The uninformed perceive all stamps to be potentially valuable, so boasts sound credible and with the passing of time, gain luster.

A dealer friend once remarked, with regard to legacies of misinformation, that: "You can't argue with a ghost." And, indeed, it's true. The Bates collection is a good example.

Mrs. Bates invited me make an offer on her late husband's stamp collection. They had married in the 1930s, started a printing business during the depths of the Depression, built it into a going concern over the years, and raised a family. She had pitched in to help build the business, working long hours alongside her husband. Mr. and Mrs. Bates had been deeply in love. Their marriage lasted nearly half a century. They had worked hard and prospered. They had lived the American dream.

Mrs. Bates was in her early eighties when I met her on the day I came to see her late husband's stamp collection. She was frail and had an insubstantial quality about her not unlike an ember that glows only in a draft. The Bates collection filled more than 20 large cartons. I found no rarities, but a broad range of moderately priced material from all over the world housed in a multitude of specialty albums. I could tell from the way he had painstakingly mounted and described his stamps on artistic, handmade pages that Mr. Bates had enjoyed his stamps immensely.

As I leafed through the albums, Mrs. Bates reminisced about the circumstances surrounding the acquisition of an item or the winning of an award. "Ned started that collection during the war," she said, referring to an album of patriotic cachets. "He was so patriotic." Her eyes lit up and her face brightened as she related the story; the love she had had for Mr. Bates was as apparent as the love he had had for his stamps. Mrs. Bates talked animatedly. The events splashed and sparkled in the telling, suddenly alive again in the bright sunlight of those cloudless yesterdays.

"He started that collection soon after we were married," she said, referring to a Monaco collection. "The stamps are so colorful, so beautiful. Ned loved art so much. That's why he collected Monaco. He appreciated the beauty of the stamps, said they were miniature works of art. We didn't have much money in those days," she recalled wistfully, "but we were young. Ned and I both worked long hours—all day from early morning until late at night, nine or ten, 'till whenever the work was done."

As she spoke, it was as if Ned lived again, and they were young once more. The energy and enthusiasm of her words melted away the years, and even her frailty faded. The moments—full, happy, wonderful times—danced in her eyes. The words flew eagerly from her lips like caged birds suddenly freed.

"Work was hard to get in the Depression. Ned made the sales calls and I ran the shop. We worked and worked—oh, how we worked. Competition was stiff. Everyone wanted the best possible price so our margins were very low, but we made it. We succeeded because we went out of our way to please our customers. They got the very finest quality, and Ned was very proud of that. Nothing ever went out of the shop unless it was first rate—absolutely first rate. Satisfaction guaranteed." I found it easy to visualize the energetic entrepreneur and his devoted partner, the hard times, the hard work, the long hours, the scramble for business, the attention to detail, the pride in workmanship. They had shared a good life.

"Ned won an award for that collection just before he passed away," Mrs. Bates said as I began leafing through an album of Antarctic stamps and covers. Then suddenly she choked up, tears came to her eyes. She reached into her purse for a handkerchief, but she could not seem to stop the sniffling. "Please, forgive me," she said. "We had so many wonderful years together." It was easy to see how much she missed him, and I felt a wave of sadness wash over me. "I'm so silly," she said, wiping away a last tear.

"The albums are lovely," I said, trying to comfort her. "Ned was a very meticulous collector."

"Thank you," she replied, struggling to be cheerful, but her eyes were red, and her face drawn under the strain of fighting back overwhelming sadness.

I spent several hours on the evaluation, hours that proved to be an emotional roller coaster—alternating episodes of smiles and tears. Morning stretched into afternoon. Time and again, I stopped to hear the story behind one item or another. I could have finished in much less time, but I paused out of respect and sympathy whenever Mrs. Bates recalled an episode.

"Ned was so excited when he got that cover. Franklin D. Roosevelt autographed it," she said, tapping it with her finger. "It was just about the time our first child was born." Each time she spoke, the memories blazed as fresh and bright as the day they occurred. Then, just as quickly, they evaporated, bringing the present—as pale as the winter light that streamed in diagonal shafts across the dining room table—sharply back into focus. Again and again she dabbed at her eyes, but the tears would not be stanched. Her joy in the past, in the years she and Ned shared, was as intense as her grief in the present, in the knowledge that those times were now gone forever.

Finally, all the albums had been evaluated and all the stories had been told. Mrs. Bates fell silent. She seemed monumentally sad under the weight of all those decades. The collection represented a powerful reminder of Ned and their happy years together. Ned had loved his stamps; Mrs. Bates had derived her joy from his pleasure and happiness. Her stories revealed her strong emotional attachment to it, and I questioned whether she would be able to part with it. I even wondered why she wanted to sell it. It was clear that she didn't need money. In any case, the time had come to talk business.

"The collection is worth about fifteen thousand dollars," I said. A look of surprise flashed across her face, then she choked up as if I had said something unimaginably cruel.

"I think I'll keep it for the time being," she managed at last, her voice full of resignation.

We sat silently for a long moment. Then I asked, "Is it the price?" I wanted to know why she had suddenly decided not to sell.

"Yes. It's much less than I expected," she replied, tucking the tissue she had been clutching into her purse. I was curious to know her figure. I had evaluated the material carefully and made a reasonable offer.

"What price did you have mind?" I asked.

She remained silent for a long moment, as if debating with herself whether to reveal the figure or let the matter drop. Finally she spoke: "Fifty thousand dollars."

I was astonished. Fifty thousand dollars was far beyond the value of the collection at full retail. It puzzled me because it was so completely unrealistic.

"How did you arrive at fifty thousand dollars?" I asked. Again she was silent for a long, long moment.

"Ned told me the collection ought to be worth fifty thousand," she answered at length.

Our two figures were so far apart that it was obvious we would not do business. Still, having invested so much time in valuing the collection, I wanted to know how Ned had arrived at $50,000.

"Do you know how he arrived at that figure?" I asked.

She reached for another tissue. After she'd wiped away more tears, she continued, "In the hospital, just before he passed away, Ned told me that the collection ought to be worth fifty thousand dollars. He said that he had collected stamps for fifty years, and the collection ought to be worth a thousand dollars a year. That's all I know about its value—just what Ned told me as he lay there in the hospital." She fought back another wave of tears.

Ned had not collected for investment. He had not kept track of his expenditures. He had no way of knowing how much he had spent over the years, and since he had never contemplated selling, he had never taken the time to calculate his collection's value. Instead, he had only a vague notion of its value, and his wife had no idea at all. As the end drew near, he tried to give Mrs. Bates some idea of its value, but it was a shot in the dark. She took his word as Gospel. And as my friend had pointed out, I found that I couldn't argue with a ghost.

"Well, I can't argue with Ned's opinion," I said, wanting to explain to her how I had arrived at my offer. "And there's no question that the collection holds a lot of sentimental value for you. Unfortunately, I have to value stamps on their merits, on what I can afford to pay and still expect to make a reasonable profit. The fact is, I'd be extremely lucky to get half your asking price at full retail."

Coldhearted as it may sound, Ned Bates should have advised his wife how to go about determining the collection's true market value instead of pulling a figure out of thin air. Or he should have had an appraisal done before he died so that his wife would have an objective figure to work with rather than a vague, visceral figure offered up from his death bed. The real value of the collection was far different than Ned's gut-level estimate. Although he had given Mrs. Bates a figure in order to help her, it would only prove to be an obstacle. Before I left, I suggested that she might want to get other offers in order to satisfy herself as to the real market value of the collection.

She called six weeks later. She said that she would consider doing business at $30,000. She had taken my advice and gotten another offer, although she didn't say how much it was. I declined her $30,000 offer, reiterating that it was far above reasonable market.

More weeks passed. Then, again, she called. She asked how much above $20,000 I'd be willing to go. I explained that $15,000 was the maximum I could pay. I had figured the lot fairly and I was not inclined to raise my offer. I advised her to take a higher offer if she had one. Our conversations were painful because she could not discuss the collection without resurrecting emotionally charged memories.

As the weeks dragged on, I began to lose interest in the collection. It's been my experience over the years that collections are most appealing when first viewed and that their appeal tends to diminish with the passing of time.

We didn't speak again. About a year later, I learned that she had sold the collection. The information came to me third hand from a dealer who knew a dealer. According to him, she had received other offers in the $12,500-$15,000 range. The collection had finally changed hands for $15,500. My offer had been bumped by $500.

After struggling with Ned's ghost for more than a year, she had finally sold the collection. In the lengthy process, she learned that

Ned's deathbed figure had been, in fact, just off the top of his head. Ned had not intentionally misled her, but he could have spared her a lot of trouble and grief. At last, tired of shopping offers, she had sold the collection for $500 more than her next best offer, which had been mine. Ironically, had she taken my offer the year before and invested the $15,000 invested at even 5 percent, she would have received $750 in interest and been $250 ahead.

This advice is not confined to just the elderly: advise a family member of the nature, scope, and *realistic* value of your stamp collection. Misinformation only causes a conscientious but unknowledgeable executor a lot of unneeded distress. Spare heirs the trouble of counting on inflated value, and the disappointment of learning that a collection is worth substantially less than they were led to believe.

If you come into possession of a collection, understand that an objective market evaluation may vary substantially from what you may have been led to believe.

THE GAMES PEOPLE PLAY

BATMAN

Stamp buying is a competitive business. Sellers shopping for offers put dealers in the position of bidding competitively against one another. When the shopping is finished, the seller takes the highest offer, and the unsuccessful dealers never hear from him again. Usually, but not always.

In my early years in the business, I was a very aggressive buyer willing to chase a lead to the very ends of the earth if necessary. Before experience tempered my youthful enthusiasm, I approached every deal as if my life depended upon it, and I was extremely disappointed when I couldn't close one. I worked diligently to be informed. I honed my closing skills. I wanted collections, and I knew that I had to be competitive to get them.

Back in the late 1970s, I got a call from a real estate broker who wanted to sell the stamp collection he had inherited from his father. The realtor lived in the Polo Club, a very exclusive, upscale neighborhood in Denver. As soon as I heard the words "Polo Club," I visualized a million dollar collection.

Instead, it turned out to be an accumulation of mint sheets. Although the bulk of it was discount postage, it contained just enough better sheets—such as the Famous Americans set, the airmail transport set of 1941, and the 80-cent Diamond Head airmail—to make it interesting. The realtor's father had purchased only well-centered sheets and stored them carefully in mint sheet files. They looked as fresh as the day they had been printed. It wouldn't be a high profit lot, but there was money to be made in the premium sheets. I gladly would have purchased them separately had the realtor not insisted that the accumulation be sold intact. I didn't relish the chore of getting rid of the discount postage.

I counted up the sheets and offered $2,800. I estimated that there might be as much as $700 profit in the lot—if I was lucky. If not, there would be less.

The realtor thanked me for my offer and said he would be in touch. In order to be prudent, he wanted to get at least one other offer. I was eager to buy the lot and disappointed at not being able to close the deal on the spot. Before I left, I extracted a promise from him that he would call if the other offer was close to mine.

Several days passed. Then on Saturday afternoon he phoned. "You said you wanted an opportunity to match any other offer," he began. I was pleased to hear from him and anxious to learn about the other offer. "There are two gentlemen here right now who have just offered $2,900. Can you top their offer?"

The news took me aback. I assumed that he would call me after he had gotten other offers, not in the middle of negotiations. My immediate reaction was that he was lying, that there were no dealers in his home. I thought it was a ploy to get me to raise my offer.

"How do I know there are two other dealers there? What do you take me for, a fool? I'm not bidding against phantoms."

"There *are* two dealers here," he insisted. But I was not convinced.

"I made an offer in good faith. Now I'm supposed to believe that two imaginary dealers—right there in your home at this very moment—have topped my offer? And you want to know if I'll top theirs? I'm not bidding against imaginary competitors. It's just not the way I do business," I said angrily.

"But there *are* two dealers here," he insisted. "I can describe them." He described the first man. It didn't ring a bell. "The other guy is in his fifties. Dressed in a gray suit." The vague description did nothing to allay my suspicions. "And he's wearing white tennis shoes."

"White tennis shoes" hit me like a bolt of lightning. Instantly, I knew the realtor wasn't lying. Two dealers were in his home, and one of them was Batman.

Batman liked to act as a silent partner in stamp deals. He didn't have a stamp store. He was more like a hired gun—always ready to assist in appraising, closing, or financing a deal for a piece of the action. He was experienced, knowledgeable, shrewd, and resourceful. He kept a low profile, staying out of sight until a deal was at hand. Then he'd appear out of nowhere, close the deal, and disappear just as quickly—hence the nickname Batman. He had one telltale quirk—he wore white tennis shoes with business suits. Batman prided himself on his closing ability, liked to boast that he never came across a deal he couldn't close. He'd snatched more than one deal out from under me, and he was in the realtor's home that very minute ready to seize yet another one.

"Okay, I believe you," I said. "I'll give three thousand for the lot."

"Hang on just a minute." The phone thumped as the realtor set it down. I heard his footsteps recede and strained to hear the conversation at the other end of the phone, but couldn't make out the words. My adrenaline was pumping. I don't know whether I was more angry at the realtor, at Batman, or at myself for going along with the game.

"They've offered thirty-one hundred," the realtor said, returning to the phone.

"I'll go thirty-two hundred," I replied.

Again the phone thumped down and the realtor walked off. The resale value of the lot was perhaps $3,500, tops. I'd likely lose money if I had to pay $3,400, taking into account the time it would take to work up the lot. I wondered if Batman would bid $3,300. I debated whether to offer $3,400. Normally, I would have walked away from the deal, but I didn't want to let Batman get the collection. I wanted to beat him. But was it worth foregoing a profit or even taking a loss for the privilege? Yes! Then, no! I couldn't make up my mind. Adrenaline pumped. I struggled with the decision. If I bid $3,400, would Batman go $3,500? I knew what the stamps were worth and guessed that he wouldn't. At $3,500, he'd be buried. What to do? My heart raced. Then the moment of truth arrived; the realtor came back on the line.

"I guess you've bought yourself a collection," he announced.

"They've dropped out?"

"I would say so judging from the way they just stormed out of the house." My anger turned to exhilaration, then amusement. They, too, must have decided they were being played for fools against a phantom telephone bidder. They had become just as annoyed as I had been. But the joke was on them. Without a similar telltale clue, they had no way of knowing I was not a phantom. I had almost dropped out at the beginning—and would have—had it not been for the revealing remark about the white tennis shoes.

I paid more than I had wanted to, but I came away doubly pleased; I got the collection and one-upped Batman.

GAMBIT

During the spring of 1979, a series of potential sellers stopped by my office mentioning that they had been referred by a certain coin dealer, whom I shall call Paymore Coin Company. I was flattered that Paymore Coin would recommend me.

On each occasion, the seller stated that he didn't know much about stamps, was in the market for an offer, and that I had been recommended by Paymore as a reliable dealer. And on each occasion, I valued the stamps and made an offer. Invariably, the seller thanked me, remarked that the offer sounded fair, and said that he'd get back to me when he was finally ready to sell. The Paymore referrals were typically neither large nor remarkable, and were spaced sufficiently apart so that I really didn't pay too much attention to the fact that not one single referral had resulted in a purchase. I was so busy at the time that I simply forgot about Paymore referrals once they walked out the door.

Then one day a Paymore referral came through the door with a particularly nice collection. The owner seemed anxious to sell, yet once I made an offer, he hemmed and hawed. I persisted, trying to close the deal. I had made a reasonable offer, and I wanted to know why he had suddenly become reluctant to sell.

"Have you gotten other offers?" I asked.

"No, yours is the first."

"How many other offers do you plan to get?"

"Probably just one more."

"I'd like the opportunity to match or beat it. Will you give me a shot?"

"I don't know," he said, frowning, then adding, "Might not do much good." He appeared uncomfortable.

"Oh, why?" I persisted, curious about his answer.

"Look, the guy at Paymore Coin told me to come over and get an offer from you. He said you were very knowledgeable and honest, that you would give me a fair offer. He told me that he was just getting into stamps, and he needed collections badly to build his stock, so whatever you offered, he'd top it." He lowered his eyes and avoided my gaze.

Suddenly Paymore's scheme became clear. Let me do the work, then outbid me by a few bucks. At that moment, I realized that I hadn't bought a single collection referred by Paymore Coin despite the numerous offers I had made. So much for Paymore Coin's altruism.

"Well, you've got my offer. If Paymore'll give you more, go ahead and sell to them," I said, suddenly not really caring to do business with the man anyway. He picked up his stamps and shuffled out. At least I was wise to the game.

The next Paymore referral introduced himself as Mr. Ridley. He reminded me of a TV anchorman—dressed like a *Gentlemen's Quarterly* fashion plate, personable, outgoing, eager to talk about the portfolio of investment coins Paymore had created for him. At the time, early 1979, double digit inflation had created a whirlwind market for tangibles and coins were red hot. Mr. Ridley had fallen under the spell of coin and precious metals gurus. In fact, the way he gushed about precious metals, you might have thought he was a precious metals salesman.

He allowed that he might be interested in selling his stamps—if the price was right. But the moment he mentioned Paymore, I knew that he had no intention selling to me.

He'd brought in an impressive selection: mint U.S. commemoratives complete from the Columbians to about 1930, including all the key high values; Washington-Franklins, again with key values; the 1922 definitive series; the Presidential series; the first airmails; and the 1930 Zeppelin set. All housed in a small, high-quality German stockbook, the kind with clear plastic pockets. A second stockbook contained stamps of Israel, including the key sets with tabs.

We chatted. He knew he had quality stamps, but said he hadn't been following the stamp market too closely—except that he'd heard stamp values were way up. I assumed that the purpose of getting my offer was to facilitate a trade of stamps for coins at Paymore. I felt certain that he had no intention of selling to me, regardless of how much I offered. I looked the stamps over, muttering praise about their scarcity, condition, and his good taste. He basked in the praise as if it were sunshine.

"Eighty percent of catalogue for the U.S.," I said when I had finished, "is the best I can do." Then I added apologetically, "I wish I could offer more." In fact, the key items—attractive as they were—had all been either regummed or reperforated. As such, they were worth perhaps 25 percent of catalogue—at most—even in the bull market.

"The best I can do on the Israel group is sixty-six percent of catalogue," I continued. That, too, was about triple what the stamps were worth. In cash terms, the offer amounted to more than $30,000. "I wish I could offer more," I said again. In fact, I had just offered him far, far more than he could expect to get anywhere else. Oddly, the offer didn't seem to faze him. He just nodded thoughtfully, as if seriously considering it.

Finally he said, "I understand. I think I'll hang on to them for the moment . . . but when the time comes, I'll keep you in mind."

"The market is extremely volatile right now," I cautioned. "My offer expires the moment you walk out the door." I gambled that he wouldn't take it, and I didn't want to be called upon later to honor it.

He nodded perfunctorily, confirming my suspicion that he never had any intention of selling to me. Anyone who knew values would have grabbed the offer and run. Instead, he thanked me and left.

I felt sure that my offer would be used as the basis for negotiations at Paymore Coin. However, both Ridley and Paymore were in for a big surprise. Ridley might quote my offer truthfully, or he might exaggerate it. Either way, it was an offer Paymore could not possibly meet. If they did, they would lose money—a lot of money. If they declined, they would lose face. Either way, they would certainly conclude that Ridley had grossly exaggerated my offer in order to take advantage of them.

If Paymore Coin made an offer based on the real value of the stamps, which was only about one-third of what I had quoted, Ridley would assume that they were trying to cheat him. The seeds of dissension had been sown. Both parties would suspect one other of trying to pull a fast one.

I only wish I could have been a fly on the wall to learn what happened. Whatever the outcome, I felt that both deserved what they got. I never saw Ridley again, and happily, referrals from Paymore Coin dried up as well.

CHECKMATE

Here's one last anecdote about competitive bidding to round out this chapter.

"I'm wrapping up my father's estate," the caller said. He was a physician who had come in from out of town to settle his father's affairs. "It's quite an extensive collection. If you're interested, please come over and make an offer. I want to wrap everything up by tomorrow evening so I can get back to Cleveland." He described the collection briefly, as best he could without having any philatelic knowledge. It sounded as if it would be worth a look. "Can you come over this afternoon?" he asked.

"I can be there in half an hour," I replied. "I'm leaving right now."

On the way out my office door, I ran into a dealer acquaintance, whom I'll call Checkers. Checkers asked me where I was going. I told him that I was on my way out to look at a collection.

"Out in Littleton?" he asked. I replied that it was.

"Doctor settling an estate?" Again, I replied in the affirmative.

"I was out there this morning," he volunteered. "Lots of material, but mostly run-of-the-mill stuff. Didn't really interest me too much. I figured it was worth about fifteen hundred dollars," he added nonchalantly. "Too much run-of-the-mill material. You'll see when you get there." And with that, he turned and hurried off as if late for a pressing engagement.

Although it's not like a competitor to reveal how much he has offered for a collection, I didn't give it much thought because Checkers was naturally talkative. Perennially cheerful, he simply couldn't keep quiet. He loved to share tidbits of gossip or regale you with details of his latest big deal. Even when the deals weren't big, he exaggerated them so that they sounded as if they were. He was one of those individuals who is always more impressed by his exploits than anyone else is.

As it turned out, the collection did contain quite a bit of rather ordinary material: later mint and used United States; post-1945 mint sheets and plate blocks; first day covers back to the mid-1930s; plus a lot of miscellaneous stamps of the type that look like they ought to have value, but really don't. It was just as Checkers said—run-of-the-mill. But then most collections are. Still, there is a profit to be made on every collection if it can be bought.

I totaled my figures. They amounted to $2,100. At $1,500, I assumed that Checkers must have rushed through the collection or wasn't seriously interested in buying it. I could have bumped his offer by $100, but I prefer to quote them as I see them.

"I can give you twenty-one hundred dollars," I said.

"Fine," the doctor replied. "One more dealer will be looking at the collection later today. I'll let you know if your offer is the best after this last fellow's been here." We shook hands and I left.

Later that day, at about five o'clock, he called back. "I'll take your offer."

"Great, I'll be out in the morning to pick it up, if that's convenient." He indicated that it was. Then on the spur of the moment, I asked, "If you don't mind telling me, how much was the second highest offer?"

"I don't mind at all. It was eighteen hundred, fifty dollars," he said, then mentioned the dealer's name—Checkers. Suddenly it became clear why Checkers had been so eager to volunteer information about his bid and to disparage the quality of the collection. He must have assumed that I would bump his offer by $100 or so rather than take the time to calculate the tedious volume of material. Had I done so, his offer of $1,850 would have bought the collection. Checkers had not counted on me doing my own homework. Unfortunately for him, he had guessed wrong.

I picked up the collection the next morning. While I was making out the check, the doctor remarked, "You know, that other fellow, Checkers, called back last night to find out if his offer was highest. When I told him it wasn't, he seemed surprised. He asked who had made the highest offer and by what amount. I told him. He sounded apologetic and said that he must have overlooked something. Then he said that he knew I wanted to get the best price possible and, therefore, would top your bid by $50. I declined. I told him I couldn't do that, that I had already accepted your offer. He was persistent though and, in my opinion, unethical."

No question about it—Checkers was unethical. He had attempted to trick us both. He had given the doctor a low bid, then tempted me with phony information. That failing, he tried to buy the collection out from under me. In the end, he had nothing to show for his scheming.

I never let on to Checkers that the doctor had told me about his chicanery. In fact, the next time I saw him, I rubbed it in. "Boy, that collection you passed up turned out to be a real gold mine."

"Really? Well, it wasn't for me—too much run-of-the-mill material," he replied without his usual bravado, trying to brush my remarks off as if the collection had not really mattered to him, but I knew differently.

Don't get the idea that every transaction is riddled with intrigue; 99 percent of all transactions are utterly routine. The point is that you should remember that stamp dealing is a competitive business. Stamp dealers know that every time they make an offer, they are competing against other dealers. They know full well that it is in their own self-interest to make the best offer possible—and that fact benefits the seller.

HAIL TO THE CHIEF

"How would you like to fly out to Palm Springs and take a look at Gerald Ford's stamp collection?" the voice on the telephone said. It belonged to Frank Trumbower, then president of Scott Publishing Co. He was calling from New York. At the time, I was vice president of Scott Philatelic Corporation, a subsidiary headquartered in Denver, Colorado. Scott Philatelic was in the business of buying and selling stamps and collections.

"Are we talking about *the* Gerald R. Ford?" I asked.

"One and the same," Trumbower replied. "He called just a few minutes ago. Apparently he's got a stamp collection, and he wants to sell it. It's at his home in California. Rhonda's got all the information. I told him you'd call him back."

The news was, indeed, surprising. No one was aware that Gerald R. Ford collected stamps. After I had finished speaking to Frank, his executive secretary, Rhonda, came on the line. Young, bright, energetic, vivacious and capable, Rhonda possessed a gregarious sense of humor. She was quick on the uptake, and like many who live in Manhattan, operated with more than a level spoonful of skepticism, a quality that evidenced itself as she related the initial Ford phone call.

"This guy calls and claims to be President Ford. Says he wants to talk to someone about selling his stamps. So I said, 'Sure. Who is this really?' But he insisted that he was President Ford. I just knew someone was trying to play a joke on me, so I kept asking him, 'C'mon now, who is this really.' But he insisted that he was Gerald Ford. I mean, like, Gerald R. Ford is just going to pick up the phone and call Scott. His secretary or assistant might call, but not Gerald R. Ford in person.

"I was about ready to say, 'Look, Bozo, if you don't tell me who you are, I'm hanging up,' but thank God I didn't. And the only reason I didn't is because I thought it might be one of Frank's friends. Finally, I buzzed Frank and told him there was some clown on the line who claimed to be President Ford.

"You know," she continued, "Frank didn't believe him either at first—but it really was Gerald R. Ford. I feel like a complete fool. I will say this—he was a good sport about it. Can you imagine being a former President of the United States, yet no one will believe you? I'm so embarrassed. I can't believe I almost flamed him off."

At length, Rhonda explained that the stamps were at the Ford residence in Rancho Mirage, located about a dozen miles from Palm Springs. She gave me a private number to call to arrange an appointment.

I called. President Ford's secretary in Rancho Mirage was most cordial. I wasn't sure how to refer to Mr. Ford since, by that time, he had been out of office several years, but she assured me that protocol dictated that he be addressed as President Ford—so President Ford it was. She described the collection as voluminous, but could offer no particulars. She suggested that I spend two days at Rancho Mirage, one day to appraise the collection and the following morning to meet with President Ford. We made an appointment for midweek about three weeks hence. She asked me to call back once I had made plane reservations so that she could have someone meet me at the airport in Palm Springs.

I spent the next three weeks wondering what I would find in Rancho Mirage. Franklin D. Roosevelt's stamp collecting interest was well-known, but the philatelic community was unaware that Gerald R. Ford collected stamps. What does a President collect? From whom does he buy? Would I find items in his collection such as the elusive die proofs (trial impressions of printing dies) FDR was so fond of? The questions dashed around and around in my head like horses on a racetrack without a finish line.

The day to fly to Rancho Mirage finally came. The flight from Denver to Los Angeles seemed to last forever. In Los Angeles, I hopped a commuter flight to Palm Springs and spent the entire time worrying about whether I would have enough time to properly evaluate the collection. I had no idea how large it was or what it contained. The only thing I had to go on was the initial, vague remark about it being voluminous.

I checked my attaché case several times to make sure I hadn't forgotten anything: legal pads, two calculators, a complete set of Scott catalogues (which I don't normally take on appraisals; however in this case, I wanted to be prepared for any possible eventuality), stamp tongs, watermark fluid, business cards, and sample auction catalogues. Everything appeared to be in order.

The plane arrived about noon. I wasn't sure who would meet me at the airport. However, no sooner had I entered the small terminal than two men in casual clothes approached and identified themselves as Secret Service agents. Outside the terminal, one of them handed me the keys to a Chrysler LeBaron and instructed me to follow their car.

After a brief drive, we arrived at the Ford compound in Rancho Mirage. The complex gave no clue to the identity of its resident. Surrounded by a large, sand-colored stucco wall, it blended perfectly with the California desert. A small guard booth stood at the end of a long driveway. It reminded me of a parking attendant's shelter, but it was manned by a Secret Service agent who monitored everyone entering or leaving. The entrance itself was blocked by a black, crashproof iron gate that sealed off the compound from the outside world.

The lead car stopped at the gate. Its driver pointed back to my vehicle. The gatekeeper nodded and the gate rolled open. Inside, the lead car pulled into an angled parking space. The agent who had been driving walked back toward me, a walkie-talkie in hand and an Uzi submachine gun slung over his shoulder. I asked him where to park as the black gate rolled shut behind me. "Just park anywhere," he answered, pointing to a row of spaces, "and leave the keys in it. No one's going to bother it," he added with a smile. One look at the Uzi left no doubt in my mind that he was right.

Stepping into the Ford home was like walking onto the set of a James Bond movie. Everything looked bright, new, elegant. The seal of President of the United States was woven into luxurious, deep-blue carpeting that lay at my feet in the entryway. A dozen secretaries worked at a flotilla of desks occupying a large open space that stretched off to one side. The understated clack-clack-clack of well-oiled IBM typewriters filled the air. The

well-dressed staff worked purposefully, efficiently. Other staffers
came and went, moving quietly among the typists, picking up
papers and dropping off others, paying no attention to me. *Yes,
just like something straight out of James Bond,* I thought to myself.

"May I help you?" the receptionist asked, bringing me back to
reality. I gave my name and mentioned that I was there to look at
the Ford stamp collection. "Yes," she said, "we've been expecting
you." She picked up the phone, and a moment later, another
woman appeared and showed me down the hall to a conference
room. It was dominated by the largest conference table I had ever
seen, and its walls were covered with photographs of world leaders
and celebrities. Most of the photos were autographed. I wondered
if the conference table had been at the White House, and if so, how
many of the personalities whose photographs adorned the walls had
discussed important matters of state around it.

"Let me know if you need anything," the woman said, closing
the door, leaving me alone. Stacks of albums covered the
enormous table—before me lay the President's stamp collection.

For a moment, standing there all alone, I couldn't believe where
I was. Of the thousands of stamp dealers in the world, fate had
chosen me to make the appraisal. When I started out in the stamp
business those many years before, never in my wildest dreams had
it occurred to me that someday I would appraise the stamp
collection of a President of the United States. It was the thrill of
a lifetime.

The stacks of albums appeared to be in no particular order, so
I just chose a spot and started. I took great care to examine, note,
and value each item. Soon my yellow legal pad contained pages
and pages of notes. I wanted to be ready to answer even the most
trivial question accurately.

Working my way around the table, I came across a beginner
album, the kind that kids used to be able to buy for a dollar. Like
all beginner albums, it contained pages of common used stamps.
The stamps had been mounted by a youngster, who like all
youngsters, was happy to have them just the same. The youngster
had written his name proudly on the front page: Gerald Ford.
Funny how many of those lowly dollar albums have introduced
people to the joys of stamp collecting. I made a note on the legal
pad: beginner album—$5.

Next to Gerald Ford's humble beginner album lay a stack of royal-blue leatherette cases, each stamped in gold with the Presidential seal. Each album contained a complete sheet of commemorative stamps mounted by the Postal Service for presentation to the President. *Now that's the way to collect new issues,* I thought.

I continued working my way around the table. The collection contained a wide range of material, much of it historical rather than purely philatelic. Autographs of Apollo 11 astronauts Neil Armstrong, Buzz Aldrin, and Michael Collins graced an otherwise common "First Man on the Moon" first day cover. Another first day cover, circa 1948, bore the autographs of Harry and Bess Truman. I came across a Barbero missile mail cover addressed to Congressman Gerald R. Ford.

I worked steadily. The fourth wall of the conference room was a floor-to-ceiling plate-glass window that provided an abundance of desert sunlight. The window looked out onto a terrace and swimming pool. Beyond the pool stood the large, sand-colored stucco wall and to the left of the pool, a well-manicured putting green. Occasionally, one or two casually dressed Secret Service agents making rounds strolled past the wall across from the pool. They looked like Saturday afternoon golfers, except for the walkie-talkies on their belts and the ubiquitous Uzis slung over their shoulders. *Not much need for burglary insurance,* I mused.

The afternoon flew by. At times, I worried that I might not be able to get through all the albums. There were so many. I worked steadily, made dozens of pages of notes, and in no time at all, five o'clock rolled around. I laid down my pen and let out a deep breath. I was finished. The Ford collection would not be the largest, the most valuable, or the most philatelically impressive collection I would ever appraise, but it was certainly the most memorable. It contained no great philatelic rarities, no gold-medal-winning assemblages of 1847s or 1869s, nothing exotic or unusual. What struck me most about it was that it was the type of collection enjoyed by the average collector, the kind of collector you meet at stamp shows and clubs all across America. It was not a royal collection, like that of Queen Elizabeth, filled with exceptional rarities that few ever see. Instead, it was filled with unpretentious stamps like those millions of people enjoy; it was an everyman's collection—and that impressed me.

The following morning, I reviewed my notes carefully as I sat alone with my thoughts in the conference room waiting for Gerald R. Ford to arrive. It's not every day one makes a presentation to a former President of the United States.

Then, just after ten o'clock, the door opened and a tall, fit-looking man dressed in casual clothes strolled in, a pipe in one hand. He smiled, extended the other hand, and said, "Hi, I'm Jerry Ford." He didn't introduce himself as Mr. Ford or President Ford, but simply as Jerry Ford—he could have been the guy next door. I shook his hand and introduced myself. His friendly manner put me at ease right away.

"Tell me about my stamps," he said. "Do I have anything worthwhile here?" I started at one end of the table and progressed around it album by album, referring to my notes as I went. I shared my opinion on each item. He nodded and asked questions occasionally. Now and then, he shared an anecdote about a particular item.

"I got these stamps when I visited Red China," he said, paging through a bright-red, silk-bound presentation album emblazoned with a large crest of yellow stars. The album contained a year set of nominal value, but it was nonetheless impressive.

Soon we arrived at his boyhood album. "These stamps aren't worth too much," I explained. "Perhaps five dollars."

He flipped through it. "My first album," he reminisced. "Started it when I was just a kid. Stamps really fascinated me. Sure brings back a lot of memories." What is it about our first album that holds so many fond memories? He took a puff on his pipe and continued. "My kids just aren't interested in stamps. I accumulated all these over the years," he made a sweeping motion toward the table, "with the thought that someday they would be interested. But they don't have the slightest interest." There was a note of disappointment in his voice. It was a story I had heard many times before. Lots of people put stamps away for their children or grandchildren who, it turns out, simply are not interested.

"Well sir, you should probably hang onto it," I said, referring to his beginner album. "It's really not worth much."

"You're right," he replied and set it aside. "It's got a lot of sentimental value." Gerald R. Ford impressed me. He was straightforward and unassuming, not like so many of the egotistical, self-important, pompous politicians of lesser stature that I had met over the years.

We continued going over the albums. At one point the door cracked open. A secretary peeked in and said, "Excuse me, sir. Senator Goldwater is on the line."

"Tell him I'll get back to him in a while," President Ford responded. I couldn't believe my ears. It was November 1980 and Ronald Reagan had just been elected President. I could only guess at what matters Senator Goldwater wanted to discuss, perhaps cabinet appointments or high-level Republican politics. In any event, it would have to wait until the stamp session was finished.

"As I've said," he continued, "the kids just aren't interested in stamps, so I'd like to auction them off and have the proceeds benefit the Ford Library and the Eisenhower Medical Center." I listened and nodded. "What do you think the collection is worth?" he asked finally.

"Well, sir, it is easy to estimate the philatelic value but I think the collection will yield substantially more because it belonged to a President. The extra value—the celebrity value, if you will—is difficult to estimate. I would prefer to give you a conservative figure based on just the philatelic value. Anything above that will be a bonus."

"Fair enough," he said. "Now tell me about your company's auction terms." I outlined our terms and conditions, and explained how the collection might be lotted. When I had finished, he smiled and said, "Okay, let's do it." I was thrilled.

"Say, I'd like to show you something else if you've got the time." What a question! Of course, I had the time. Besides, who could resist an invitation like that. He led me to his private office and from the large bookshelf that covered one wall, pulled out a book entitled the *Warren Report*. "I served on the Warren Commission, you know," he said. I hadn't remembered. The Warren Commission investigated the assassination of John F. Kennedy. He handed me the large volume, his personal copy of the Warren Commission report. I opened it. The flyleaf was covered with autographs. It could have been a high-school yearbook, except for the names—Earl Warren, Allen Dulles, Senator Richard Russell, Lyndon B. Johnson, Representative Hale Boggs, and other prominent political figures of the time.

His office was filled with memorabilia of decades in public life: medals, photographs, and so forth. He pointed out several, pausing to tell the story associated with each. A gigantic photographic enlargement—a breathtaking scene shot from space—covered the far wall of his office. I admired it again and again as we chatted. At one point, I mentioned how my two sons, Steve and Mike, were wild about anything space-related. "It's a NASA photo," he said. It turned out that Gerald R. Ford, too, was fascinated by space exploration.

The morning passed quickly and then all too soon, it was time to go. I had a plane to catch and Gerald Ford certainly had more pressing matters. However, I left with the impression that he would have been just as happy to pass the afternoon chatting about stamps and collectibles.

About a week after I got back to Denver, a large envelope from Rancho Mirage arrived in the mail. It bore the free frank of Gerald R. Ford. It contained a personal note of thanks and several autographed NASA enlargements for the kids. How very thoughtful this gentleman was.

We auctioned the Ford collection months later on September 16, 1981, at Grand Rapids, Michigan, Gerald Ford's hometown. Prices realized astounded me. The auction grossed more than four times my original estimate. Someone made the remark that each of the party faithful in attendance wanted a souvenir—and the spirited bidding seemed to bear that out. I bid $750 for the Neil Armstrong autographed first day cover, but it sold for more than $1,000. To this day, I regret not having bought it. It would have been the perfect memento of one of my most thrilling philatelic experiences—the Gerald R. Ford collection.

SURPRISE, SURPRISE, SURPRISE

After you've been in the business long enough, you end up seeing the same old stamps time and time again. And although you enjoy seeing them and handling them, it's the people and the situations that provide freshness and stimulation to what otherwise quickly becomes a very routine business. Each seller and each situation—especially those encountered away from the office—is an adventure. You never know what you will find.

I arrived at the Harms residence early one afternoon. It was a modest home with a two-car garage located in a quiet suburban neighborhood. It was the kind of home that resembles all the other homes on the block, completely unremarkable in every respect. Mrs. Harms had insisted that I come to her home. Her late husband's collection was simply too massive to bring to the office.

I really didn't mind. In fact, I looked forward to getting out of the office. It was late May, I had a case of spring fever, and visiting Mrs. Harms offered an opportunity to get out into the warm spring sun, if only briefly.

Initially, the collection proved to be as unremarkable as the house. Nothing more than dozens of stockbooks containing tens of thousand of recent U.S. commemoratives soaked off paper. It was the kind of collection that keeps you hoping desperately that the next stockbook will contain the good stuff, while intuition tells you that you have already seen the best it has to offer.

"My husband liked to soak stamps and sort them," Mrs. Harms explained as I flipped through the stockbooks. That much was apparent, judging by the sheer number of stockbooks that she retrieved from closets, nooks and crannies, lugged to the kitchen table, and piled in front of me. No question that the late Mr. Harms had spent a lot of time soaking and organizing stamps. The problem was that they were all recent commemoratives, the type for which packet makers pay 25- to 35-cents per hundred.

It was not the kind of collection dealers dream of finding. Its value lay in its sheer bulk. It would be a great lot for a packet maker, which I was not. I questioned whether it was worth the trouble to prepare for shipment and sale to someone who was.

"What do you think it's worth?" Mrs. Harms asked when I'd finished.

"A few hundred dollars, I suppose," I said with a wrinkled brow, still trying to get a handle on it.

"Oh, I've already had an offer of much more than that," she replied. "I've had an offer of nine hundred fifty dollars."

The figure was patently ridiculous. Despite its bulk, it was worth nowhere near $950. Still, her words had the ring of truth. After you have purchased enough collections, met enough sellers, heard enough stories, you can tell when someone is telling the truth, bluffing, or exaggerating. You acquire the ability to read people, an important asset because you discover early on that if you believe everything you're told, you soon go broke. I had no doubt that Mrs. Harms had been offered $950, but I couldn't figure out why someone would offer so much.

"Did a stamp dealer make that offer?" I asked. It occurred to me that perhaps someone completely unfamiliar with market values had made the offer.

"Oh, yes, it was a dealer," she replied matter-of-factly.

Then I had a thought. "Have you shown me everything? Left nothing out?"

She thought for a moment, then turned and headed for the kitchen closet. From it she produced a stack of folders that contained several hundred dollars worth of mint sheets.

"I'm sorry. I forgot about these," she said. The mint postage was worth more than the stockbooks of used stamps, yet even with the mint stamps the value didn't come to $950.

"Is there anything else you haven't shown me?"

"Only the stamps out in the garage."

I was not prepared for what I found in the garage. If you read comic books as a youngster, you're probably familiar with Walt Disney's Uncle Scrooge. Uncle Scrooge hoarded money and stored it in a money bin resembling a swimming pool, complete with diving board. Uncle Scrooge's comic book friends dived and frolicked in the coins and bills. What I found in the garage reminded me of Uncle Scrooge's money bin. It was a stamp bin.

Mr. Harms had constructed the stamp bin smack-dab in the middle of their two-car garage. There was no room left to park cars. The bin stood four feet high and measured perhaps eight feet on each side. It had been made of sheets of unfinished plywood braced at the corners. I rummaged around in the stamps, grabbed a few handfuls, but saw nothing except common definitives. I didn't find a single commemorative. *Now this is an item for the collector who has everything,* I thought. A person could dive in and bury himself in stamps, just like the characters in Uncle Scrooge's money bin.

The only way I could even begin to place a value on the stamp bin was to visualize a one foot cubic box, estimate the number of pounds of stamps that would fit in such a box, and then estimate the number of boxes the bin might contain.

"They're pretty common," I said, turning to Mrs. Harms, a handful of stamps slipping through my fingers like sand. "They're not worth much."

"I didn't think so," she said. "He sorted through mixtures and soaked off the good stamps. But he just couldn't bear to throw the rest away, so he made this bin and dumped the leftovers in it. I'd like to get it out of here so that I can park the car inside." I could see her point.

Including the stamp bin, I figured the whole lot to be worth $1,000. The other offer was reasonable. My figure was barely more. The accumulation offered little in the way of profit potential: lots of labor-intensive packet material, a bunch of discount postage, and the stamp bin. Novel though it was, the more I thought about the stamp bin, the less I liked it. It would take a truck to move the stamps. And where to store them? What to do with them? They were ultra-common.

My usual impulse is to close a deal, but sheer bulk—coupled with low profit potential—made this deal unappealing. So I made an offer I knew Mrs. Harms could refuse. "The whole works looks like about nine hundred dollars," I said, praying she wouldn't accept it. "You should take the nine hundred fifty dollar offer. It's more than fair."

"Couldn't you go nine-fifty?" Mrs. Harms asked. "If you'll match the other dealer's figure, I'll let you have it." Unfortunately, I didn't want to buy it.

"No, I'm sorry. Your best bet is to take the nine-fifty offer. It's really not the kind of material I can use," I said, more sure by the moment that I had made the right decision. Let the stamp bin be someone else's problem.

I later learned that the other dealer had bought it. Still, every once in a while, I wonder what it would have been like to dive into the stamp bin and thrash around. Then I think, *Don't be silly, you're not a kid anymore!*

As I've said, stamp buying is an adventure. You never know what you're going to find at someone's home or place of business. Often you're surprised—sometimes unpleasantly, but equally often, pleasantly. So it was at the Nellises.

A dozen albums, more or less, stood neatly arranged in the old steamer trunk, the kind made obsolete by the age of jet travel. The Nellis sisters, Vera and Elizabeth, explained that the albums had belonged to their late father, who had been an avid collector. He had died the previous year, and the trunk-full of stamps was one last bit of unfinished business.

Vera and Elizabeth Nellis were seated, backs straight as West Point cadets, on a sofa behind the coffee table. I was seated at the end of the coffee table.

"Would you care for a cup of tea, Mr. Datz?" Vera asked pleasantly, but precisely. The room reminded me of a Victorian parlor, crowded with furniture and knickknacks. It would have appeared cluttered except that everything was in its place, perfectly and precisely. The precise metronomic tick-tock of a grandfather clock keeping watch in the corner completed—enhanced—the sense of order. Sixtyish, the Nellis sisters were prim and proper, and one got the impression that their lives were as neat and well-ordered as the room, as precise and smooth running as the well-oiled grandfather clock.

"Yes, thank you," I replied. "No sugar, please." Vera poured the tea carefully until the cup was just three quarters full, then she poured Elizabeth's, and finally, her own. The Nellis sisters struck me as genteel, women from the bygone era of the steamer trunk.

"Many's the night Dad spent working on his stamps," Vera reminisced. "He liked to settle in after supper—especially on cold winter nights—and spend the evening poring over his albums." Elizabeth nodded in agreement. "I'm afraid we don't know much about stamps," Vera continued. "None of us ever really developed an interest in them."

As we chatted, I learned that there were four sisters: Vera and Elizabeth, who had never married, and two others who lived out of state with husbands and families.

"We thought we might just divide the albums among the four of us—three albums for each," Vera explained. "The collection may not be worth much, but it has a lot of sentimental value to us. We thought we might divide it so that each of us could have a memento of Dad. However, we'd like you to give us some idea of it's value," Vera said. Then putting her hand on the China teapot, she asked, "More tea, Mr. Datz?"

"No, thank you," I replied, thinking how very pleasant an appraisal could be. The Nellis sisters were delightful hostesses. Their hospitality sure beat leaving a mobile home with curses ringing in your ears.

The steamer trunk of albums sat beside a large oak table near the front window. The table offered plenty of work space and the window, lots of light—little things greatly appreciated by anyone who has had to examine stamps in poor light or crowded conditions.

The collection contained two albums housing U.S. mint singles, a number of others devoted to cancellations and viewcards, and a couple of stockbooks containing duplicates and miscellaneous. Mr. Nellis had mounted his stamps neatly on handmade quadrille pages, carefully identifying each one. All too often, one finds inexpensive stamps incorrectly mounted in spaces meant for the expensive varieties, but not in the Nellis collection. Every stamp was in its proper place. Nor had the late Mr. Nellis tolerated faulty stamps; all were first-rate. The collection was correct and straightforward, formed with the same care and neatness that bespoke the room and bearing of his daughters, the Nellis sisters.

The best album contained early material, including a variety of mint Columbians, Trans-Mississippis, Panama Pacifics, and the like, up to the two-cent reds. The next best album contained a collection of used stamps that paralleled the mint stamps of the first album, although it was not as complete. The other albums contained viewcards, groupings of interesting but common cancels, and miscellaneous stock of relatively little value.

"Well, ladies, I have some good news for you," I announced when I had finished. Judging from Vera's remark about the collection being of nominal value, I was sure that they would be pleased with my appraisal. "The collection is worth ten thousand dollars," I said. "I can give you a check for that amount right now."

However, their reaction was not what I expected. "Oh, my," Vera said, putting her palms to her cheeks in amazement. "Ten thousand dollars?" She looked shocked.

"Yes, ma'am," I said. "Your father put together a quality collection. I am prepared to write you a ten-thousand-dollar check for it."

"Oh, my," Vera repeated, looking at Elizabeth. "We had no idea it would be worth that kind of money. Are you sure?"

"Yes, ma'am." The Nellis sisters looked at one another, seemingly at a loss for words.

"Oh, dear, I don't know what we should do," Vera said. Elizabeth said nothing.

"Perhaps we should just divide the albums among us, three for each sister," Vera thought aloud. Events were not taking the course I had expected. I had assumed they would welcome my offer, that they would accept it on the spot because it was so far above their expectations.

"What do you think, Mr. Datz?" Vera asked. Of course, I thought they should sell the collection to me, but it was not for that reason alone that I pointed out the inequity that an album-by-album division would create.

"Dividing the albums might not be wise," I said. "One album is worth about eight thousand dollars, another is worth about seven hundred fifty dollars, and the balance of the value is spread among the other ten albums, some of which are not worth even fifty dollars. If you divide the albums, one of you will do very nicely and the other three will come up short—very short."

"I see," Vera said. "That does present a problem."

"Selling the collection would solve the problem, allow you to divide the value fairly," I suggested. "Unless sentimental value is an overriding factor."

"Yes, I suppose it would," Vera said slowly as if deep in thought. Elizabeth remained silent, her face filled with uncertainty.

"I had no idea the collection would be this valuable. We should probably let Shirley and Marian know," Vera said, turning to Elizabeth, who nodded in agreement.

My optimism turned to pessimism. I knew from experience that the more complicated a transaction becomes, the less likely it is to turn out satisfactorily. The married sisters would have opinions, their husbands would have opinions, and suddenly, the collection would represent a treasure. Perceived value has a way of growing all out of proportion to reality. I could just hear the reasoning.

"If he's willing to offer ten thousand dollars, someone else might offer fifteen or twenty thousand." Such is the unwritten rule to which the uninformed often subscribe. The logic and greed of the rule dictate that a dealer in stamps, coins, antiques, or whatever, only ever offers a very, very small fraction of an item's true value. The real value is always much greater than what the dealer offers—so the rule dictates. There is no way to argue with greed. Greed has a quality about it as compelling as youthful infatuation, a quality that utterly possesses the mind, fevers it with visions of imaginary wealth.

I sensed that the collection was slipping, like a handful of melting snow, between my fingers.

"Oh dear, Mr. Datz. This is truly startling news. We had no idea the collection was so valuable," Vera said once again. "I'm afraid we're going to have to talk it over with our sisters." Elizabeth nodded in agreement. "I don't know what we'll do."

"You have my card and my offer. I would like to buy it, and selling would solve the problem of dividing the value equitably. You could each keep one of the less valuable albums if sentimental value is important," I said. "Please, let me know what you decide to do." I thanked them for the tea, bid them farewell, and left assuming that I would not hear from them again.

About two weeks later, Vera called. "Is your offer still open?" she asked.

"Yes," I replied, surprised to hear from her. I assumed that the collection had been set up on by greedy relatives, like jackals on a fresh kill.

"Good," Vera said. "We've decided to take you up on it. The collection is just as you left it. You may pick it up at your convenience."

"I'm curious to know why you decided to sell it," I said. "The day I visited at your home, I got the impression you wanted to keep it."

"I'll be frank with you, Mr. Datz," Vera said. "We had decided to sell the collection before you made the appraisal—if it was worth more than a couple of hundred dollars. We doubted it would be. We assumed that it was worth little, and that we would end up dividing it up among ourselves. In fact, had you offered $200, we would have sold the collection right then and there. We had no idea it was so valuable. Naturally, when we learned of its great value, I felt we should consult our sisters before we did anything. After all, it was their property, too."

Despite the explanation, I found it odd that they would have accepted $200 for the collection and not given it a second thought, yet rejected an offer of $10,000. The episode confirmed, once again, that every stamp buying transaction is an adventure—an adventure in which one learns to expect the unexpected.

'TIS THE SEASON

Earlier, I mentioned that most stamp collections do not come to market as distressed goods. However, occasionally it happens.

It was a blustery, gray December afternoon, the kind kept cold and damp by low overcast, the kind that brings darkness prematurely to an already abbreviated winter day. Late that frigid afternoon, a well dressed, middle-aged woman and her son, who appeared to be about twelve, walked through the front door of my office suite. They were red-cheeked and bundled up against the cold. The woman carried a heavy, black sample case, the type used by sales representatives.

I ushered the visitors into my private office and hung their coats while they rubbed their hands together. I offered them seats in front of my desk. The woman introduced herself as Mrs. Bergman. Her son's name was Kevin. Kevin craned his neck to get a better view out the sixth floor window behind me. Beyond the glass, in the gathering gloom, tiny cars crawled along snowpacked streets. Here and there, city lights had just begun to wink on.

"I'd like to get an offer on this collection," Mrs. Bergman said in a businesslike tone as she pulled the first album from the black case and placed it on my desk. It was a green Scott National album, the type so familiar to every stamp dealer. But unlike those usually encountered, it contained a multitude of key items: Columbians, Trans-Mississippis, a White Plains souvenir sheet, lots of Washington-Franklins, Zeppelins, and many others—all mint. It appeared to have been assembled before 1960. It contained few stamps after that date.

As I paged through the album, young Kevin leaned forward in his chair, elbows on my desk, and spoke to his mother in short, animated, but hushed bursts. "The Zeppelins," he said as I passed that page. Mrs. Bergman nodded silently at each remark. Kevin clearly enjoyed showing off the stamps. In fact, he could hardly sit still as he anticipated each new page.

Other albums followed one by one. The collection impressed me. It had been put together the way a collection ought to be: clearly focused, few extraneous duplicates, with an eye toward completion. As I paged through it, I shared my appreciation aloud. "Very nice . . . very nice." Kevin beamed at each compliment, but Mrs. Bergman only nodded slightly and smiled politely. I saw no joy in her eyes.

After I had totaled my figures, I set about explaining how I had arrived at the offer that I was about to make. Mrs. Bergman listened attentively. When I had finished, she spoke. "I really don't want to sell the collection. It was my father's and I had hoped that my son would have it someday," she said, turning to Kevin. Kevin's enthusiasm for stamps—that special, intense enthusiasm only youngsters have—was obvious. From his remarks during the viewing, I could tell that he knew the story behind every stamp. He had spent many happy hours with the collection. Mrs. Bergman's remark about not wanting to sell it did not surprise me. Her silence and discomfort during the viewing were as telling as Kevin's enthusiasm. Then, before continuing, she told Kevin to go out and wait in the reception area.

"Do I have to?" he complained, as if just having been told it was time for bed.

"Yes," his mother said gently but firmly. She seemed pained at having to send him away. "Run along until we finish," she said, trying to be cheerful. When he was out of the room, she continued in a tone as gray and somber as the December sky outside. "We owned and operated a restaurant for many years. It was a successful business and a good living. About a year ago, we were forced to sell it. My husband developed cancer, and the time came when he could no longer run the restaurant. I couldn't handle it by myself and care for him at the same time—and we needed the money for medical expenses that just went on and on."

Mrs. Bergman was a slender woman in her late thirties whose slight appearance seemed to belie her inner strength, but courage and quiet determination were evident in her eyes and in her voice.

"The man who bought our restaurant couldn't pay cash, couldn't even put much money down, but he was the only one who would give us what we thought the business was worth, so we carried his note. To make a long story short, not only did he stop making payments a few months later, but he ran the business into the ground—sucked it dry. He ran up debts and didn't pay them. He has long since disappeared, and I am now in the position of having to take it back or lose everything. My husband died in September. I still have a mountain of medical debts."

It is never pleasant to hear about the misfortunes of others. Mrs. Bergman's tale was no different. She had lost nearly everything, including her spouse and her business, and now she was about to lose yet another valued possession—her father's stamp collection. As I listened, I wondered if she had she enjoyed the stamps as a youngster, pored over them at her father's elbow, relished them as much as young Kevin did. The collection was clearly rich in sentimental value and especially difficult for her to contemplate selling given Kevin's attachment to it.

At that point, Kevin reappeared at the door, having grown restless in the waiting room. Besides, he knew well the purpose of the trip. "Mom, do we have to sell the stamps?" he asked plaintively. I could see that he hoped—as only a youngster can hope—that the answer would be no.

"I'm afraid so," Mrs. Bergman said as courageously as she could. The air hung heavy with emotion. I feared Mrs. Bergman might lose her composure at any moment. "Now go on, wait outside until I'm finished," she urged.

"Aw, Mom, can't we keep some of it? Do we have to sell it all?" Kevin pleaded. He was not about to let it go nor was he about to leave the room, and his entreaties were making a difficult moment even more painful. Resolute as she was, I wondered how long Mrs. Bergman could retain her composure.

Suddenly, I wanted very much for it to be no longer necessary for her to have to sell the collection. I wanted her to be able to pick it up and walk out with it. I wanted her to be able to take it home and hand it to Kevin with a smile and say, "Here, it's yours. Enjoy it!"

It was getting late. Beyond my window, the afternoon was dying. Its grayness had deepened into charcoal, and the lights of the city sparkled on the winter landscape like a dusting of incandescent snowflakes.

"Much as I hate to part with the collection, I need the money to get the restaurant going again and pay off some of the more pressing bills," she said, focusing on the matter at hand.

I offered $7,500, which she accepted without comment. I pulled the checkbook out of the drawer. Then I had a thought. "You should probably keep this one," I suggested, pointing to the album containing later material. The bulk of the collection's value was in the albums containing earlier material.

"How will that affect the price?" Mrs. Bergman asked. "I need every dollar I can raise."

Although I had figured the album for $400, I replied, "It won't affect the price at all. Here, I want you to keep it." I separated it from the others and handed it to her. "It's not really worth much, so you might as well keep it," I said untruthfully. I had a feeling that if she had known how much it was really worth, she would have refused to take it back.

Kevin reappeared at the door. Mrs. Bergman motioned him in and handed him the album. "This is for you," she said.

"Gee, Mom, this one's got a lot of neat stuff in it." He grabbed it and held it to his chest, swaying back and forth as if hugging a long-lost friend. I hoped he would keep it forever.

"Thank you very much," Mrs. Bergman said quietly, gratefully. Then, "If I could have a check for the rest of the albums, I think it's time we headed for home." Kevin sat in the chair next to his mother, paging through the album as I made out the check.

Christmas was only a week away, and watching Kevin leave with the stamp album tucked under his arm delighted me as much as any gift I could have wished for. It was five o'clock when they left. I stood at my window. On the sidewalk six floors below, I could see Kevin and Mrs. Bergman making their way toward their car. It was completely dark outside, but the gloom was gone. The winter scene below struck me as festive. The city sprawled before me, adorned by countless thousands of twinkling lights celebrating the bright, cheerful holiday season. *Enjoy your stamps,* Kevin, I thought, as they pulled away from the curb and drove off into the sea of lights. *Enjoy your stamps—always.*

SUMMARY

SELECTING A DEALER

Select a reliable dealer. It's your best insurance for getting a good price. Do not hesitate to ask for references, the length of time a dealer has been in business, or professional credentials such as membership in the American Stamp Dealers Association (ASDA). Upon request, the ASDA will provide a list of member dealers in your area. Not all stamp dealers are ASDA members. Many completely reliable dealers are not members.

Sell to the best market for your particular collection in order to obtain the best price. Just about any dealer will be in a position to pay you a good price for a general collection, either U.S. or foreign. If you have a specialized collection, consult a specialist.

METHODS OF SALE

Methods of sale include outright sale, auction, consignment, private treaty, donation, and gift.

CONDITION

Condition is the key factor of value. Sound stamps are priced according to grade. Prices vary substantially from grade to grade. Faulty stamps trade at very low percentages of catalogue value. Faults include tears, thins, holes, creases, scuffs, and the like. Stamps with pieces missing are virtually worthless. Regummed, reperforated, altered, or "restored" stamps also sell for a small fraction of catalogue value.

Do not attempt to separate stuck-together stamps or to remove stamps from album pages. You may damage them and reduce their value. Leave those tasks to experienced professionals. Do not attempt to clean stamps. Do not remove stamps from envelopes or postcards; intact envelopes may have much more value by virtue of their postmarks or other markings.

STAMP VALUES

Stamp values are determined by the stamp market, by supply and demand. Each stamp is priced according to its merits and generally, the more expensive the stamp, the less the markup. Many variables are involved in stamp pricing, so stamp catalogue values serve only as reference points, not absolutes. Actual values vary—often substantially—from catalogue value.

Beginner collections—on which a few dollars were spent—are usually not worth much. Valuable collections are typically formed over decades by methodical individuals who have spent meaningful sums of money on better than average items. Post-1945 mint sheets usually sell at a discount from face value. Sentimental value is owner specific and not transferable—it has no value in the marketplace. Albums, supplies and labor generally have no resale value. The actual cash value of a collection is only as much as the best offer for it, no more.

Don't automatically assume that your stamps are the rarest possible varieties. Read the stamp catalogue—including the introduction—carefully and check your stamps thoroughly. Remember: "All that glitters is not gold."

APPRAISAL

An appraisal is a valuation by an expert. In most cases, an appraisal is a formal, written evaluation for which the owner pays a fee. Stamps are appraised in two ways, either for replacement value (typically for insurance purposes) or market value (estates, legal settlements, etc.). Replacement value is the amount one would expect to spend buying at retail. Market value is the amount one would expect to receive selling to a dealer.

Appraisal fees are charged by the hour or as a percentage of the net appraised value. A minimum fee—typically $25 to $100—usually applies regardless of the value of the collection. Most dealers refund appraisal fees if they end up buying the collection.

Always have an appraisal done by reliable professional. The ASDA can provide you with a list of member dealers in your area.

OFFER

An offer is the cash price a dealer will pay for your stamps on the spot. An offer is based on a variety of factors including the dealer's circumstances and attitude toward the stamps. Offers tend to vary, although for routine stamps—such as general U.S. and worldwide collections—they are usually fairly close to one another. As a general rule, you'll get the best offer from a dealer who has immediate need for your stamps. Two or three offers will usually give you a pretty good idea of what your stamps are worth.

Some dealers will not make free offers, especially if they think you're insincere about selling. However, for a fee, they will usually agree to make an appraisal. The fee is usually refundable should you sell to them.

SELLING BY PHONE OR MAIL

Selling by telephone or mail gives you access to every dealer in America. From these, you should have no trouble finding a dealer who meets your needs. As mentioned, ask for general and bank references, years in business, and professional credentials such as ASDA membership. Reluctance to use the mails can severely limit your ability to get the best price, especially if you have specialized material.

A telephone call is only a preliminary. In most cases, dealers won't quote prices over the phone without first having seen the stamps. Dealers are often willing to travel to buy valuable collections—the minimum value is usually $5,000 to $10,000. If your collection doesn't meet the minimum, the dealer may suggest that you ship it for an evaluation.

Organize information about your stamps before calling. Dealers tend to be selective about which calls they choose to follow up because most collections don't amount to much. The dealer will need specific information in order to make a decision about whether to travel to your home, ask you to ship your stamps for an offer, or recommend some other course of action. Be prepared to provide the following: general size, scope, age (old vs. modern), mint or used, general condition, value (if known) and basis (catalogue, purchase receipts, etc.).

When making an inquiry by mail, send an inventory if you have one. If not, send the most detailed description possible per the guidelines above. However, don't expect a firm cash offer based on an inventory. The inventory serves only to establish interest. The dealer will need to see your stamps in order to make a cash offer. If you're not willing to ship your stamps for an offer, don't waste time writing to dealers—no one buys stamps sight unseen. Large dealers—especially those who get a lot of mail inquiries—often will not respond unless they're definitely interested or unless the inquiry is accompanied by a self-addressed, stamped envelope (SASE). Be sure to include your telephone number; a phone call saves a lot of time.

Don't send dealers samples from your collection. Samples tell little. It's just not possible to generalize the value of a collection from a sample. It is necessary to see the whole collection in order to get an idea of its value.

SHIPPING

Ship stamps by registered mail and insure for adequate value. Registered parcels may be insured up to $25,000. Don't use certified mail; it has no insurance coverage. Pack your shipment securely and use paper tape. The U.S. Postal Service will not accept registered parcels sealed with plastic tape. Always include your telephone number and the best time of day to be reached.

Agree in advance who will pay return shipping and insurance if the offer is not acceptable. Get a commitment in advance as to how soon after receipt the dealer will evaluate your stamps and how quickly payment will be made if you accept his offer. Immediate payment is standard. Avoid installment payments.

TRAVEL

Some stamp dealers travel, but only if they feel a collection justifies the expense of the trip, *and* only if they feel they have a good chance of buying it. The cost of airfare, hotel, and auto rental does not permit wild-goose chases.

Do not expect a dealer to travel unless you are prepared to do business or unless you are willing to pay his expenses. If you have no notion of your collection's value or how much you want for it, get an appraisal, or select a dealer in whom you have confidence and whose offer you will feel comfortable accepting.

GETTING TO YES

When it comes time to talk business, be straightforward, direct, and businesslike. Don't hesitate to state your asking price. Remember, dealers base their offers on the market, their own needs, and a property's profit potential, not on whether you need money, what you've got in it, a bluff, or a hypothetical test. These and other irrelevant arguments only create an atmosphere of insincerity and mistrust. They distract from the useful, essential elements of negotiation which are: the market value of the stamps, what you want for them, and whether a dealer's offer is competitive. Sincerity and good faith are essential to mutual respect in any transaction. A sincere approach is usually met with a sincere response. Dealers like nothing less than sellers who insist on playing games. Remember, stamp dealers meet the public every day; they've heard every story in the book.

If you want an appraisal, say so. If you want an offer, say so. If you intend to get other offers, say this as well. If you know how much you want for your stamps, don't hesitate to state your figure right up front. Establish a rapport with a dealer, if possible. Not only will it make the transaction more pleasant but potentially more profitable as well.

SELL IT ALL

Avoid selling piecemeal. In almost all cases, the best price is obtained by selling a property intact. When a collection is sold piecemeal, the choice items invariably sell quickly, but it is usually difficult to get a good price for the balance. The premiums received for the choice items do not offset the discounts subsequently levied against the remaining stamps. The premium items are the dealer's incentive to purchase the whole lot.

ERRORS

Errors require a special strategy because their value is so time-sensitive. If you find an error, move quickly and quietly. Seek out and work with a specialist in the error field. The error market is extremely quantity sensitive. Be careful about how much noise you make shopping your find. You don't want to create the impression that more copies of the error exist than actually than do. That impression will make potential buyers nervous and only serve to drive the price down.

Dealers don't like to gamble on newly discovered errors until it becomes fairly clear how many are out there. The possibility of others surfacing always exists. This is especially true for definitive stamps, which are typically in production for a period of several years. The moment more surface, an error's value falls. Because the market is so quantity-sensitive, holding a newly discovered error is a risky proposition. Holding an error for the long term makes sense only if you control all known copies. Realizing a greater profit from holding long term is the exception rather than the rule.

INVESTMENT

Hold a collection for investment only if you feel its future value will be more than the future value of its proceeds if they were invested elsewhere. Remember, most stamp collections are not investment grade.

SELLING OVERSEAS

Selling outside the United States can be profitable but is not recommended for the one-time seller. Too many pitfalls exist for the non-professional: language barriers, local laws and business customs, local grading and condition customs, local taxes, and the difficulty of legal recourse in a foreign land—to mention a few.

ESTATE PLANNING

This advice is not just for the elderly. Advise a family member of the nature, scope and estimated value of your collection. If you're not sure, have an appraisal made. Be realistic in your valuation. Giving an inflated or exaggerated value serves no purpose. Misinformation only causes unnecessary distress to the conscientious but unknowledgeable executor. If you come into possession of a collection, be prepared to get an objective market opinion, and understand that it may vary substantially from what you may have been led to believe.

GLOSSARY

approvals: selections of stamps sent by mail, usually inexpensive singles or sets for the beginning or general collector. The collector purchases what he likes and returns the balance.

backstamp: a postmark placed on the reverse of a cover to indicate its arrival date or time.

bisect: a stamp cut in half (often diagonally) and used as one-half the face value of the uncut stamp.

blind perforations: incompletely or partially impressed perforations, often barely indented into the paper and giving stamps the appearance of being imperforate. Stamps with blind perforations are not considered imperforate errors.

block: four or more stamps arranged in a rectangle.

B-O-B: back of the book. Includes stamps such as postage dues, special deliveries, parcel posts, etc.—anything listed in the rear of a catalogue following definitives and commemoratives.

booklet pane: a small sheetlet of stamps bound between card-stock covers by staples, thread or glue.

bourse: a show (or section of a stamp exhibition) devoted to booths from which dealers sell their wares to the stamp-collecting public. Bourses are often held in conjunction with stamp exhibitions.

cachet: (ka-shay). A decorative illustration printed, drawn or rubber-stamped on a cover, usually in connection with the first day of issue of a new stamp or some other special event. Usually occupies the left side of the cover.

cancel: an obliterating mark applied to a stamp, thereby rendering it invalid for future use. Cancellations may be applied by handstamp, machine, or pen.

canceled to order (CTO): cancellations applied by governments, often to full sheets. CTO stamps are often sold by governments in bulk to packet makers, approval dealers, etc. CTO stamps are generally not as desirable as genuinely postally-used stamps.

catalogue: a reference work that lists, illustrates, and prices postage stamps. Stamp catalogues can be general or specialized.

catalogue number: a number assigned by catalogue publishers to identify each separate stamp listed in the catalogue. Stamps that appear outwardly the same but differ in perforation, watermark, etc. are each considered to be a distinct collectible variety. Each variety is assigned its own catalogue number, despite the fact that they share the same design. To avoid having to publish an illustration of the underlying design with each variety, catalogue publishers assign an identifying number (as distinct from a catalogue number) to each design and make reference to it with the individual catalogue listings. The identifying number usually appears to the right of the catalogue number in the listings.

centering: the position of a stamp's design in relation to the perforations or edges of a stamp. Well-centered stamps possess even margins all around.

cinderella: a general, all-encompassing term applied to any stamp-like item not valid for postage, such as exhibition labels, Christmas seals, and the like. Anything that looks like a postage stamp but is not.

classic: an early issue, usually nineteenth-century.

coil stamp: stamps issued in rolls. Coils contain straight-edges on two parallel sides.

commemorative: a special stamp issued to honor a specific event, personality, anniversary or occasion, typically on sale for only a limited time.

commercial cover: a cover used for business correspondence (although more recently any cover of a non-philatelic nature) without any philatelic intent, as opposed to one created for some philatelic purpose.

cover: a philatelic term for an envelope, almost always implying that it has gone through the mail.

cut square: a piece containing the postage imprint cut from postal stationery, usually to facilitate mounting in an album.

definitive: a stamp, usually part of a series, available over an extended time for use on everyday mail. Also known as a regular issue.

duck stamp: a waterfowl-hunting stamp.

EFO: errors, freaks and oddities. A term applied to stamps with random minor production irregularities such as misaligned perforations, shifted colors, printing offset on reverse, ink smears, etc. See *major error.*

essay: an unadopted stamp design, either an entire design not used or a design very similar to the issued design except for small modifications.

expert certificate: a certificate issued by an acknowledged expert or expertizing body attesting to the genuineness or non-genuineness of a stamp or cover.

exploded: refers to a booklet that has been dissembled into individual panes.

face value: a stamp's denomination.

fake: an outright forgery; also a stamp (or cover) that has been modified to improve its value or desirability with the intent of defrauding a buyer.

fault: any defect affecting the appearance or integrity of a stamp such as a tear, cut, crease, thin, scrape, scuff, stain, fold, pin-hole, etc.

favor cancel: a cancellation applied to a stamp or cover as a favor by a postal employee, often on an item that might not normally have been used on mail or have gone through the mail, or with a postmarking device not normally used for that issue.

first day cover (FDC): a cover—usually cacheted—postmarked on the first day a stamp is available for sale.

flat-plate press: a printing press that utilizes flat printing plates and prints paper one sheet at a time.

grill: a waffle-like pattern impressed into some nineteenth-century stamps to break their paper fibers and make them more receptive to postmarking ink. Used to prevent the removal of cancellations and re-use of stamps.

gutter: the space between two panes of stamps on a sheet.

hammer price: the price paid for a lot by the highest bidder at an auction, exclusive of the buyer's commission.

heavily hinged (HH): hinged with strong glue that has disturbed the gum or will disturb it when removed.

hinge: a small piece of paper or glassine used to attach a stamp to an album page.

imperforate: lacking perforations.

intaglio: a method of printing in which the design is engraved (recessed) into a metal plate. Ink fills the recesses and when printed forms small ridges, which can be detected by magnifying glass or by running a finger over the design and feeling the ridges.

invert: a stamp with an element of the design upside down in relation to the other elements of the design.

job lot: a mishmash consisting of just about anything, loose stamps, covers, albums pages, mixtures, mint sets, remainders, etc., often sold by the carton. Dealers often dispose of surplus, disorganized material in the form of job lots. Sometimes called a mystery lot.

kiloware: a mixture of stamps on paper sold by the pound or kilogram, hence the name.

lightly hinged (LH): hinged so that the hinge mark is barely noticeable. Implies that the gum has not been disturbed.

line pair: a pair of coil stamps on which a line appears between the stamps. On engraved, rotary-press coil stamps, lines are created by ink that fills the space where the curved plates join and is then printed in the same fashion as ink from recesses in an intaglio stamp design.

major error: usually refers to a stamp with a major production error such as a stamp lacking perforations, a stamp with a design element inverted, a stamp with a color or colors omitted, or a stamp printed in the wrong color. Minor production irregularities are referred to as EFOs. See *EFO.*

manuscript cancel: handwritten cancellation.

maximum card: a postcard bearing the same illustration or design as the stamp affixed to it and cancelled with first day or commemorative cancellation.

meter: a stamp printed by a postage metering machine such as those made by the Pitney-Bowes Company.

mint: an unused stamp with full gum as issued by the post office.

mounts: clear plastic pouches or containers used to protect and affix stamps to album pages.

multiple: a group of two or more unseparated stamps, such as a block, pair, strip, or pane.

never hinged (NH): a stamp that has never been hinged.

new issue: newly issued stamps, often received by subscription either directly from a postal administration or from a stamp dealer.

off-center: a stamp on which the design is poorly centered in relation to the perforations.

off paper: used stamps that have been soaked off paper. Most often applied to mixtures, which are sold either "on paper" or "off paper."

on cover: a stamp attached to a cover.

on piece: a stamp attached to a piece of paper torn or cut from an envelope or wrapper.

original gum: gum applied to a stamp at the time of its manufacture.

overprint: printing applied to stamps after regular production, typically to denote a special purpose (such as airmail), commemorate something, or as a control measure, etc. Overprints that change the denomination of a stamp are called surcharges.

packet: typically a printed, window envelope containing an assortment of common stamps for the beginner or general collector.

packet material: common, inexpensive stamps.

pair: two unseparated stamps.

pane: a finished "sheet" of stamps as purchased across a post office counter as distinct from a press or production sheet, which usually contains multiple panes of stamps.

perforations: the series of holes punched between stamps to facilitate their separation. The size of the holes and spacing vary from issue to issue. Perforations are measured by a perforation gauge.

plate block: a block of stamps with the printing plate number(s) appearing on the selvage. The size of the block can vary from issue to issue.

PNC: plate number coil. A coil stamp on which a small printing plate number (or numbers) appears at the bottom. Stamps with plate numbers appear at regular intervals on a roll of stamps, typically—but not necessarily—every 12, 24 or 52 stamps.

postcard: a privately produced card without postage imprinted on it and usually containing a printed greeting or view on the reverse. Often called a viewcard.

postal card: a card with postage imprinted on it by the postal service.

postal stationery: stationery sold by a postal service usually, but not always, with imprinted postage. Postal stationery includes postal cards, stamped envelopes, aerogrammes (airletter sheets), etc.

postmark: an official marking (usually circular but can be any shape, or in manuscript, or more recently, sprayed-on dot-matrix style characters) applied to a piece of mail, most often indicating date and place of mailing. Postmarks are often used to cancel stamps.

private treaty: an arrangement in which as stamp dealer acts in the capacity of agent for a seller, receiving a commission for his services.

proof: a trial impression made from a die or plate before regular production in order to check engraving, color, etc.

quadrille paper: album pages containing a light background grid (usually grey) that facilitates arrangement of stamps. Used by collectors who prefer to make their own pages.

regummed: a stamp that has had new gum applied to simulate original gum.

reperforated: a stamp that has had perforations added to a straightedge or to a perforated edge that has been trimmed to improve centering.

rotary press: a printing press on which the plates are curved in the form of a cylinder to facilitate continuous printing of a web of paper.

roulette: a philatelic term referring to a series of small slits (as opposed to round holes as in perforations) applied between stamps to facilitate separation.

selvage: the marginal area surrounding a sheet or pane of stamps. Sometimes spelled selvedge.

semi-postal: a postage stamp for which only part of the purchase price applies toward postage; the balance is collected for some other purpose, often a charitable cause. Semi-postals are usually denominated by two figures, the first applying toward postage, the second toward the other purpose, i.e. 50c+20c.

set: two or more stamps sharing a similar theme, motif or appearance, usually commemoratives, usually issued at the same time, and usually, but not always, of different denominations.

se-tenant: two or more different stamp designs printed next to one another on the same pane, souvenir sheet, booklet or coil.

short set: an incomplete set of stamps, usually comprised of only the lower denominations.

sound: free of faults.

souvenir sheet: a sheet, usually small, containing one or more stamps, usually bearing a commemorative marginal inscription, and usually issued for a special event or occasion.

strip: three or more unseparated stamps attached side-to-side or end-to end (as opposed to in block form). A roll of 100 stamps is actually a strip of 100.

tagging: a luminescent coating applied during printing. It is used to facilitate the facing and handling of mail by automated equipment. Usually invisible to the naked eye, it can be observed under ultraviolet light. Tagging may cover all or part of a stamp.

viewcard: see *postcard.*

wallpaper: common stamps with little individual value, especially brightly colored foreign pictorials. Typically issued with low face value and sold in bulk to stamp packet makers by developing nations.

watermark: a design impressed into paper during its manufacture, sometimes visible when held up to light, most often visible only when immersed in watermark fluid. Do not immerse stamps in water to detect a "watermark"; use only watermark fluid designed for that purpose.

watermark fluid: an inert liquid (that will not affect gum) used to detect watermarks. Several brands are commercially produced and available at stamp dealers.

APPENDIX

PHILATELIC PERIODICALS

American Philatelist (monthly)
P. O. Box 8000
State College, PA 16803
(814) 237-3803

Global Stamp News (monthly)
P. O. Box 97
Sidney, OH 45365
(937) 492-3183

Linn's Stamp News (weekly)
P. O. Box 29
Sidney, OH 45365
(937) 498-0801

Mekeel's Weekly and Stamps
P. O. Box 5050
White Plains, NY 10602
(914) 997-7261

Scott Stamp Monthly
P. O. Box 828
Sidney, OH 45365
(937) 498-0802

Stamp Collector (bi-monthly)
700 East State Street
Iola, WI 54990
(715) 445-2214

STAMP CATALOGUES

Brookman Price Guide (U.S.,
U.N. & Canada)
700 East State Street
Iola, WI 54990

Scott Stamp Catalogues
Scott Publishing Co. (U.S. &
Worldwide)
P. O. Box 828
Sidney, OH 45365

Errors on U.S. Stamps
Krause Publications
700 East State Street
Iola, WI 54990

DEALERS' ORGANIZATIONS

**American Stamp Dealers
Association** (ASDA)
3 School Street, Suite 205
Glen Cove, NY 11542-2548
(516) 759-7000

STAMP SOCIETIES

American Philatelic Society
(APS)
P. O. Box 8000
State College, PA 16803
(814) 237-3803

STAMP INSURANCE

**American Philatelic Society
Insurance Program**
P. O. Box 8000
State College, PA 16803

EXPERTIZING

**American Philatelic
Expertizing Service**
P. O. Box 8000
State College, PA 16803
(814) 237-3803

Philatelic Foundation
70 West 40th Street, 15th Floor
New York, NY 10018
(212) 221-6555

GIFTING

Stamps for the Wounded
P.O. Box 1125
Falls Church, VA 22041